ME AND MY FEELINGS

What Emotions Are and How We Can Manage Them

By Robert Guarino

Illustrated by Jeff Jackson

Foreword by Robert Ornstein, Ph.D.

HOOPOE

Hoopoe Books

A division of The Institute for the Study of Human Knowledge

HOOPOE

Published by Hoopoe Books
a division of The Institute for the Study of Human Knowledge

Copyright © 2010 by The Institute for the Study of Human Knowledge
Illustrations from *Me and My Feelings* copyright © 2010 by Jeff Jackson
Emotion photos copyright © 2010 by Paul Ekman Ph.D./Paul Ekman Group, LLC
Foreword by Robert Ornstein, Ph.D.

General Editors: Denise Nessel, Ph.D., and Robert Ornstein, Ph.D.

Content Standards Alignment by Brett Wiley, M.A., Education

ISBN 978-1-933779-71-3

ME AND MY FEELINGS

What Emotions Are and How We Can Manage Them

CONTENTS

Education Standards Covered by this Book (*see end of book*):

  APA National Standards for High School Psychology Curricula
  California Middle School and High School Health Standards
    (Based on the California Framework)
  California State High School Life Science Standards
  National Board for Professional Teaching Standards - Health
  National Board for Professional Teaching Standards: Adolescence and
    Young Adulthood Science Standards

Acknowledgments

    This book could not have been written without the work of Paul Ekman, Ph.D. Dr. Ekman's research and many books fully explore emotions and how they affect our lives. With his kind permission, I used many photos provided by Dr. Ekman and the Paul Ekman Group, LLC, throughout this book in order to help teens not only to recognize thoughts and feelings in themselves, but also help to illustrate that these emotions are universal. Teens will learn how these emotions help to guide, shape and control them in everything they do.

Robert Guarino

FOREWORD
Open During Remodeling

Now that's a sign you don't see very often, and for good reason. Ask anyone who has had to live in a home while remodeling was going on in the kitchen or bathroom. Most businesses just close up shop while the place is being torn up and put back together. Remodels are messy, disruptive and downright inconvenient. But that's exactly what's going on in your brain!

There was once a time when all the changes that occurred around puberty were blamed on hormones. Now, we're not letting the surge in chemicals through your body off the hook, but today scientific research reveals that a second growth spurt in the brain also contributes to the changes that occur during the teenage years. Surprisingly, the changes to a teen's brain are similar to the growth of a baby's brain in the first eighteen months of life. A massive spurt of new brain cells called gray matter occurs, and nerve cells called neurons make new connections. Then slowly, throughout the teenage years and into the early twenties, cells that don't make connections are trimmed back.

Scientists speculate that this second growth spurt aids us all in adapting to the world. It seems this is the last chance in life to learn a new skill or develop a lifelong habit easily. If you take up a new skill or keep practicing at an old one, your brain will rewire itself to support these abilities at a faster rate than at any other time in your life. No wonder the teen years are such a good time to take up playing guitar or drum, or to learn to speak Chinese or Italian! On the other hand, you want to avoid getting into some bad habits because these get wired in, too, and will be harder to change later on. Now is a really good time to learn some good habits for dealing with anger, stress, and self-control. Good habits learned now really could last a lifetime.

First, you should know that the brain's frontal lobes are responsible for self-control, judgment, organization, planning, and emotional control. These are skills many teens struggle with in middle and high school as this part of the brain matures. And, according to research conducted by Giedd at the National Institute of Mental Health using Magnetic Resonance Imaging (MRI), a number of additional unexpected brain developments occur in people from ages 10 through mid-20s. This altered the previously held belief that a person's brain was fully mature by ages 8 to 10. MRIs first revealed that the corpus callosum, the part of the brain that connects the left and right hemispheres, continues to grow until a person is in their mid-20s.

While the implications of this are not fully known, the corpus callosum has been linked to intelligence and self-awareness. Elizabeth Sowell of UCLA's Lab of Neuro Imaging found that the frontal lobes of the brain grow measurably between ages 10 and 12. The gray matter in the lobes then begins to shrink as unused neuron branches are pruned. Studies such as these continue at different research centers, and a more complete understanding of what this all means is around the corner.

While this brain remodel has its rewards, getting through this time in your life can sometimes feel very complicated and you struggle to make sense of the world around you. Maybe you find yourself wondering why you're suddenly so concerned about what others think. Maybe you find yourself wanting more privacy. Or maybe you're just trying to understand why you have to learn algebra!

New questions. New school. New styles. You're changing. Your friends are changing. But you might be able to make more sense of these changes if you have the right information.

I'm not talking about the flood of information on cable TV, radio, or the bijillion blogs and websites on the net. I'm talking about "big picture" information about what it means to be you: a human being. It's information so fundamental, we often forget to teach you about it in school. For example: what psychologists know about how we see, think, and feel; how these abilities work, how they change, grow or get stuck and how reliable they are as we try to make sense of ourselves, our friends, our relatives and the world around us. There is good, solid information readily available and scientifically validated, but a lot of people seem to be too busy to pay attention to it. It's like an open secret. And it's all about you... and me.

So, the next time you feel like you are struggling to crawl out from under the rubble of your remodeling, try to remember how great it's going to be when it is all done. Better yet, take an active role. Use the open secrets discovered in this book and others in this "All About Me" series as your hammer and nails to build the you that you choose to be.

In the meantime, enjoy this journey - it's all about you!

Robert Ornstein, Ph.D.
President, ISHK

THE CAST

The concepts in this book just can't be described without some good visuals, so here are some teens who will help to illustrate the emotions and actions covered in this text.

THE CAST

Sally
as fear

Marquis
as anger

Jillian
as sadness

Frank
as happiness

Esteban
as disgust

INTRODUCTION

"I got really sad the last time I went to visit my grandma in the hospital. I remember going down the hall towards her room at the end of the hall. I saw my uncle, and he was walking toward me. He had tears in his eyes."

"What makes me happy is when I don't hear my parents fighting and there is peace and quiet in the house."

"I get angry when my friends always ask me for my homework. Don't they want to learn on their own? It feels like that's all they like me for."

"I am happy when I get a hit while playing baseball."

"Something that disgusted me was when I was playing in the park and I tripped and fell into a pile of dog 'poo'."

Emotions like these and many others are a common and important part of our lives. Understanding our emotions can help us to become successful and healthy adults. It would be a mistake to think of emotions as only the source of drama and tension. Our emotions are a fundamental part of being a human being, and you can learn to use them to help you live better.

Try This

Look at the pictures below and match each to one of the following emotions: sadness, anger, disgust, fear, and happiness.

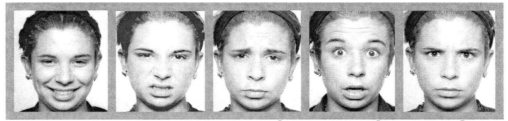

Left to right: happiness, disgust, sadness, fear, anger.

What's going on?

Emotions are universal. While different things may make us happy or sad, we all experience happiness and sadness. Some emotions may be more common among certain groups of people, but emotional expression is similar among all human groups, even those humans in remote corners of the world who have not had contact with others. Similarities have been demonstrated in blind infants, normal infants, and adults. Even the chimpanzee shares some similarities with human beings!

In humans, emotions are primarily displayed by the face. Specific facial muscles are used to create emotional expressions. Researcher Paul Ekman demonstrated that the five emotions are expressed similarly by all humans. We will explore these emotions and their specific facial expressions in later chapters.

Try This

Read the short scenarios on the next page. Associate one of the following emotions with each scenario: sadness, anger, disgust, fear, and happiness. If you can associate other emotions with each scene, make a note of these, too. Write down your answers in a notebook.

1. Sally prepares for a final exam so that she knows the material perfectly well. But when the final moment comes and the exam begins, she starts to sweat and her stomach hurts. The questions make no sense and she can't remember a thing.

2. Marquis is playing soccer at the park with a group of random neighborhood boys and girls. As the game progresses, Marquis feels he is being purposely fouled. When someone kicks him hard in the leg, he turns around and pushes the other player to the grass.

3. Esteban is babysitting his younger sister who has the flu. He thinks it will help her to feel better if she plays with the dog. Suddenly, his sister vomits on the dog. The dog starts to lick the vomit off the floor.

4. Jillian is going to a movie with some friends. Whenever she goes out, she always notices girls her age having fun with their dads. Jillian wishes she had that kind of relationship with her dad.

5. Frank has graduated middle school. He thinks, "Next year I will get to go to a new school. No more drama. New people, new friends, a new beginning."

WHAT'S GOING ON?

I associated the above scenarios with these emotions: 1 - fear, 2 - anger, 3 - disgust, 4 - sadness, and 5 - happiness.

While the five emotions listed have been widely studied by researchers, they are not the only emotions we have. Have a friend or relative read the above and do the same, then compare your answers. You may discover even more variety. Scenario #4 may provoke envy as often as it does sadness. For scenario #3, one person may react with disgust and move away when they see someone puking; another person may react with concern and move toward the person to provide comfort and caring.

Remember, different things may provoke different emotions. We all share the same emotions. We just don't always use them in the same way.

YOUR TURN

Look through a magazine or newspaper and look for emotional facial expressions. You can start by trying to find examples of the five emotional expressions common to all humans: sadness, anger, disgust, fear, and happiness. Cut out the photo and label it in your notebook. If you don't have access to magazines or newspapers, use any source that has photos - an album or textbook, but don't cut out pictures if it ruins the book! With a friend or relative, try to identify emotional expressions.

Did You Know?

Learning about your emotions can also improve your G.P.A. A recent study conducted at the University of Illinois at Chicago[1] showed that many students who participated in an extensive school program that taught them about their emotions improved their achievement scores and G.P.A.

More Fun

Make two columns on a sheet of paper. In the first column list some memories. Try for a variety of memories: some recent, some from the past, some pleasant, some not so pleasant. In the second column, write down an emotion that you can associate with each memory.

In this book we'll explore our emotions. We want to show you how and why your emotions work the way they do. Once you understand emotions, you will find them easier to manage in yourself and easier to understand in other people. This book will also introduce you to some ideas and tricks that can help you do this.

[1]Payton, J., et al. (*See References for full acknowledgment.*)

"I walked into 4th period Choir, as I do every Wednesday. As I put my stuff away, I looked up at the board and panic came over me. It was the day we were having our choir party, and the day we were supposed to return our choir blouses! I forgot to bring snacks for the party and my blouse. I was feeling anxious and guilty and worried that I was going to get in trouble with the teacher. I ran to my friend to ask her what I should do. She told me that she knew others had forgotten their blouses and that I wasn't the only one. Then I looked at the table and it was overflowing with food; there would be more than enough food without my snacks. I no longer felt bad about the food, but I was still a little worried about forgetting the blouse. Then the teacher told us that it would be fine to bring the blouses in on Friday. My friend smiled at me. I felt a lot better. I was now feeling happy that we were having a party."

- Lauren

Today:
1) Return choir uniforms
2) Semester party

TRY THIS

Think about a recent time when you were afraid. Write a description of the incident in as much detail as you can. Describe the events leading up to being scared. What facial expressions did you make? What was your breathing like? How did you react? How did this event end? Were you able to calm yourself down right away, or do you remember feeling emotional even after you realized that you were safe? If you are unable to think of a time in your life, ask a friend or relative to tell you about a time when s/he was scared.

WHAT'S GOING ON?

Emotions are automatic patterns of responding to certain situations. They are involuntary and seem to be outside of conscious control. Emotional reactions involve the **autonomic (automatic) nervous system**. Our face responds in particular ways depending upon the emotion. Our brain releases different chemicals which cause our hearts to beat more quickly or our palms to sweat. Because of these physical or **physiological responses**, we can't always calm down as quickly as we like.

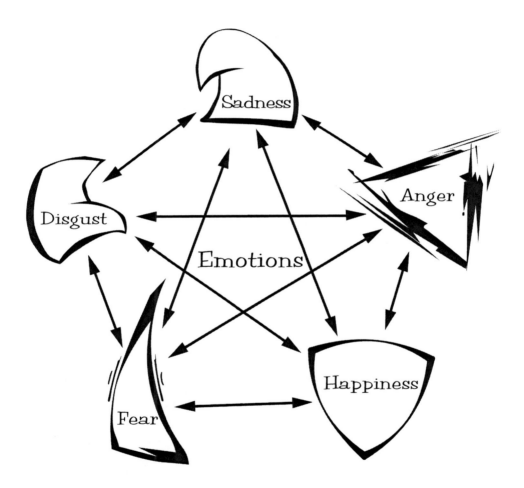

Emotions: (1) Move us to act, (2) Direct and sustain our actions, (3) Communicate actions, (4) Help organize our experiences.

Review the incident you wrote about. Can you identify the role emotions played? Did becoming scared move you to act? What action did you take? How did you communicate that you were scared? Or, did you try to hide your reaction? Were you able to identify your physical responses? How will this incident help you to organize future experiences? Will you avoid similar circumstances? Or, will you remember that there really is no threat involved?

TRY THIS

Look at the illustration below.

Write a short description of what is happening in this picture. Take into consideration the emotions of all the characters, including the dog.

What's going on?

A simple scene like the one illustrated above can clearly demonstrate the important role emotions play in our lives. It can help explain why we have emotions.

Emotions Move Us to Act

Emotions signal that something important is happening. They get us ready to respond and to defend ourselves. Emotions **trigger** a physical response in our bodies. Let's look at the scene on the opposite page. While our answers may vary, we can agree that every character has moved into action. I imagine the family has moved the dog to act to protect itself or property: it is excited, angry, or fearful. The barking dog has moved the child to react fearfully. The father has been moved to act by his child and the dog. He shows concern for the child. He may also be afraid of the dog, but he could just as well become angry with it for scaring his daughter. How might he act if he knows the dog?

Emotions Direct and Sustain Actions

Once our emotions have moved us to act, they direct the intensity and scope of this reaction. In our illustration, the excited dog has been moved to bark. How it acts will depend upon the emotion it is experiencing. If it is angrily protecting itself or its property, it will probably continue to bark, snarl, and snap at the family. If, on the other hand, it knows the family and the initial reaction was excitement and affection, it will bark but it won't snarl or snap. The child will more than likely sustain her fearful response. The child's emotions direct her to hold on tightly to her parent's leg and cry. The child may even indicate that she wants to be picked up.

The father's emotions are directing him to soothe the child. While the father's emotions are directing and sustaining him to act to care for the child, personal experiences will influence just what actions any particular person will take. How do you imagine parents would act under these circumstances? What would your parents do? Would you act in the same way? Why or why not?

But, what about the father's emotional response to the dog? That's where the final two functions which emotions serve come into play: emotions communicate actions and emotions help organize experience.

Emotions Communicate Actions

Most animals have evolved effective **display signals**, such as facial expressions, gestures, postures or odors that communicate information about how that animal is likely to act. Humans also rely on **verbal expressions**. But a dog can't speak, so the parent in the above scene will rely on his knowledge of the display signals a dog uses. If the dog is snarling, then we assume it has hostile intentions, and our emotions direct our actions accordingly. On the other hand, if the dog is barking and wagging its tail, we can assume it has friendly intentions. How is the child communicating her emotions? Let's assume the dog is friendly. Many parents would choose to calm their child by showing their child that the dog is friendly; they would go and pet the dog. Most young children will give immediate feedback as to whether or not this attempt is successful. What display signals will the child give us if it is unconvinced and still afraid? I'd bet he or she would continue to cry...and might even cry louder! What will signal that the child is calming down?

While we have been examining the emotional response of the family and dog step by step, it should be noted that all of these things happen very quickly. In real life, all that we have examined could occur in seconds.

Emotions Help Organize Experience

Our emotional state "colors" - that is, it defines or organizes - how we experience events, ourselves, and others. If the dog in the above illustration is responding angrily, it will see the family's intentions as hostile. It would be foolish for a parent to try to pet an angry dog because the dog would see any movement toward it as threatening. The dog would direct actions according to its angry emotions: it would bite the parent's hand. Similarly, if the child is scared, she is unlikely to be immediately comforted by a parent moving closer to the dog. For the child, the dog is an object of fear. The frightened child will experience any movement toward the dog fearfully.

Think about a time when you may have wanted to ask your parent or guardian for a favor. Are you likely to approach that parent if you know that they are in a "bad" mood? Have you ever decided to delay asking for a favor until a parent is in a better mood? Perhaps you have seen something like this on a television show. TV comedies will often try to get us to laugh by showing us outrageous attempts to put TV parents into "good" moods. (See Chapter 2 for more about moods.)

Your Turn

To understand how important emotions are to human beings, try to re-imagine the above scene without one or more of the important emotional functions. What would the above scene be like if the characters were not moved to act? What would it be like if the characters reacted, but their actions were not directed? What would the scene be like if the characters could not read each others' emotional display signals?

Try This

Let's examine how we communicate our emotions more closely. Choose an emotion and try to act it out. You can choose any emotion, but for this activity, choose one that you can act out easily. You have already written about fear, so you could choose to act out that incident. You may find some emotions easier or more difficult. You can do this activity alone in front of a mirror or, if you feel comfortable, with a friend or relative.

When you feel as if you have perfected your performance, observe the display signals you used to communicate what you are feeling. Did you make a face, use hand gestures, or change your body posture? Did you use any words? What did you say and how did you say it? Record your observations in your notebook.

What's Going On?

When expressing our emotions, we are using a complex system of **verbal** and **nonverbal display signals**.

Our verbal expression includes any words we may have chosen and the way we choose to say them. Some of the characteristics which can be varied are tone, volume, or speed. Look back at your notes. Did you use words in the above activity? If you didn't notice the tone, volume, or speed of your verbal expression, repeat what you said and take note of them now.

We communicate a lot through our nonverbal expression. Often we communicate more nonverbally than we do verbally. Our non-verbal behavior includes facial expressions, gestures - especially hand and foot - body posture, touch, and eye contact. Which of these did you notice in your activity? Actors on stage often have to exaggerate some of these nonverbal display signals in order to communicate clearly their emotions to the audience at the back of the theater. Replay your scene as if you were on stage. Which expressions would you exaggerate to make sure everyone knew how you were feeling?

Your Turn

Whereas actors on stage exaggerate these expressions, TV and film actors have to learn to be more subtle. We tend to criticize TV and film actors for overacting. For this, you will have to watch TV or a movie. A program that you can pause would work best. Observe an emotional scene. Identify the emotion or emotions being expressed. Make a chart like the sample below and record which display signals the actor(s) used to communicate emotions.

Now you can play director or TV critic. Rate the actor(s). How well did they do? Did they overact? Could they have incorporated more display signals? Do this with a friend or relative and compare your assessments. You may find that you have your own "taste" or preferences for acting styles.

Verbal Gestures	Nonverbal Gestures
Tone of voice Volume of voice Speed of talking	Facial gestures Hand and arm gestures Other body language

The Science

The part of the brain which gathers all the incoming information from the outside world and from the body is called the **cingulate gyrus**. It then compares all this information with as many memories as it can and sends the matched information and memory to other parts of the brain where decisions can be made on the most important ones to pay attention to, and what needs to be done next.

There are two parts of the brain that govern how the brain and the body will react emotionally to this information, and since they work together, they have just one name - the **amygdala**. They are positioned on either side of your brain near to your ears. The word "amygdala" is a Greek word meaning "almond nut" because they look about the same size and shape. Their job is to make you aware of things that may be dangerous, different, and interesting and get the rest of your mind and body mobilized. You might back away or move closer for a better look. The amygdala also play a crucial role in helping you to recognize emotions in other people's voices and expressions.

There is an area in the lower center of the brain where emotions are decided upon and generated. This area is called the **limbic system**. Two streams, or pathways, for information travel out of the limbic system, but these streams contain the same information. The limbic system sends one version down an extremely fast path straight to the amygdala to make sure that the person can take instant action if there is anything threatening in it. The same information is also sent outward by a slower path into the area around the outside of the limbic system called the **upper cortex**. This is a large area of the brain where we do our complex thinking.

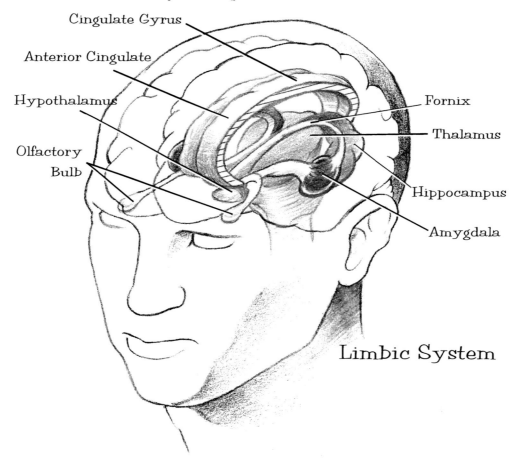

Limbic System

The amazing thing about this is that the upper cortex and the amygdala can reach very different conclusions about the same piece of information! So your emotions can fire off because your amygdala thinks something dangerous has happened, but a split-second later your upper cortex comes up with a better, cleverer idea about what is going on. Imagine being scared by a piece of rope. The amygdala would have made a fast, but crude and hasty match between the shape of the rope and that of a snake because it is primed to recognize similarity with dangerous things and doesn't need to be particularly accurate with the match between what you are looking at and its store of memories.

The amygdala's policy is "better safe than sorry." Meanwhile the upper cortex has spent a little more time on the problem and is also able to recognize the difference between a rope and a snake and can try, therefore, to calm things down if the amygdala has overreacted. This is the **involuntary response** referred to at the start of the chapter.

However, the number of connections that run the information from the limbic system up to the upper cortex vastly out-numbers the connections going the other way. The pathway upwards is like a six-lane expressway, and the pathway back is like an overgrown country lane. So sometimes it takes a while for a clearer and more accurate idea of what is going on to reach the amygdala from the upper cortex. The pulse of panic at waking in the night to find Dracula in your bedroom can effectively "drown out" the more accurate perception that it's only your bathrobe. Once our emotions are aroused, we cannot think or speak as clearly or as cleverly as we do when we are calm.

When the amygdala decides it's time for action, it sends signals to two other areas of the limbic system: the **anterior cingulate** and the **hypothalamus**. These areas then send signals into three other systems in the brain and body, making it rise to the challenge. These include:

o The release of **hormones** or **messenger chemicals** into the blood, such as epinephrine (commonly called adrenaline), norepinephrine, cortisol, or fibrogen, which helps cuts to heal (see Chapter 3 for more discussion of these messenger chemicals)

o Changes in the speed and depth of breathing

o Changes in the speed and strength of the heartbeat and blood pressure

o Changes in the digestive system

o Changes in the way blood flows out to the muscles in the arms and legs

Key Ideas in Chapter 1

Create a chart by listing the 4 Roles of Emotion (see pages 13-15 in this chapter to refresh your memory on these roles). Using one or more of the following three possible scenarios (situations), write beside each role what your response might be.

Suggested Scenarios:

1) You get put in a group at school with people that you don't know and, maybe, don't like that much.

2) Your friends expect you to win a game for the team, and you don't.

3) You receive a gift that you have been waiting for.

Here is an example of this exercise, using the third scenario, *I receive a gift that I've been waiting for.*

Role of Emotions:
Move Us to Act:

My Response: *I jumped up and down with joy with a big smile.*

Direct and Sustain Emotions:

My Response: *As soon as I saw the box, I knew what it was and I got an even bigger smile on my face.*

Help Us to Communicate:

My Response: *I gave her a big high-five and screamed THANK YOU about a dozen times.*

Organize Emotions:

My Response: *At first, I was really, really happy. Later when I calmed down, I called my friend to thank her again. I felt good about doing that, because it showed her I really appreciated the gift.*

Keep it in Mind

Start keeping an "Emotions Journal/Log." At the end of the day, log (jot down) any incident that provoked an emotional response. Make a note of the events that led up to your response. Use your chart you created above, if necessary, to help you to begin to explore the role emotions play in your life. Here is a sample:

"Today I had baseball practice. When I got there, I found out that we were going to practice our hitting. I felt happy that we were going to hit because I had been struggling at the plate. We need to get better at hitting fast pitchers. I was surprised when coach told us that we would be hitting off a tee. I was a little worried because I remember during tee ball I wasn't a very good hitter. The first time I was at-bat I just hit a slow roller to the pitcher. I was very disappointed because all the kids were saying, "Big hitter." My second at-bat was not much better, a slow roller to short but I beat out the throw. I was up again and hit a line drive up the middle. I felt a lot better that I made solid contact. Then I'm up again. Coach Rich tells me to hit it over the right fielder's head. First swing, POP, it was a shot. I stood a little to admire it. It one-hopped to the fence. It was only a triple because I caught up to Antonio who is a slow runner. It felt so good like a weight lifted off my shoulders. It was probably one of my farthest hits. It was my farthest hit off a tee and the farthest hit of the day. When I got back to the dugout my teammates were high-fiving me. It felt really good. When I was up at-bat again, it gave me a lot more confidence. I hope it travels over to the game."

-Caleb

"I was really excited because it was my friend's birthday and I had baked her a birthday cake. She thanked me and excitedly grabbed a fork along with the rest of our friends and the usual lunch crowd. Then people we knew, but weren't our lunch friends, came over and started trying to get some cake. I started to get angry because I had made this cake for my friend's birthday, not random people! Then people started commenting on how good it was and I felt proud. And I realized that there was enough cake. Then I felt stupid for being angry because it was fun talking to the people that I usually don't see at lunch."

-Lauren

TRY THIS

Look at these photos of infants and identify the emotions displayed in each.

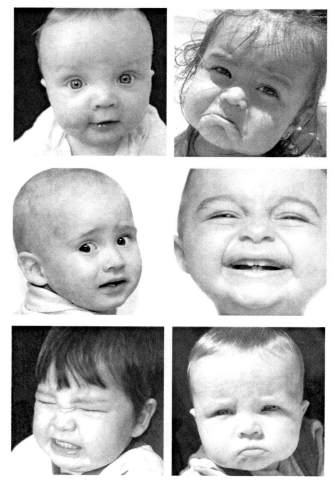

Suggested answers, left-to-right from top: 1. Neutral 2. Sadness.
3. Fear or Surprise. 4. Happiness. 5. Disgust 6. Anger

WHAT'S GOING ON?

As you probably already know, it takes several years for babies to develop the proper motor skills to learn to walk. The development of these skills occurs in a predictable order. Like motor skills, emotional expression develops naturally in a predictable sequence.

At first, infants display general excitement when emotionally aroused. The signs of this are increased muscle tension, quickness of breath, and increased movement. Over the course of the first year and a half of life, this general display is refined into specific expressions of the following emotions:

o distress   3 weeks
o anger   3 months
o disgust   3-6 months
o fear of strangers   7-8 months
o jealousy and envy   15-18 months

As most parents will tell you, crying develops before smiling. An infant cries almost immediately after being born, but most parents have to wait weeks before they see their baby's first smile!

As mentioned in the introduction, children born deaf and blind displayed the same basic facial expressions: smiling, laughing, pouting, crying, surprise and anger. Also, blind children show the same developmental pattern of smiling as sighted children.

All of this points to the universality of emotions.

Primary Emotions

Try This

Brainstorm a list of emotions. When you have a long enough list, try categorizing these emotions. Which ones are similar? How would you label each category? Here is a short list to get you started: Joy, Agitation, Disappointment, Alarm, Contentment, Amusement, Disgust, Annoyance, Bitterness, Euphoria, Friendliness, Horror, Loneliness, Paranoia, Sorrow, and Worry.

WHAT'S GOING ON?

The scientific community has not settled on one system for classifying emotions. Everyone agrees that emotions combine in different ways to make complex emotional experience. This complexity is the reason why there are many theories about the origins of our emotional experience. However, there is general agreement about identifying six basic emotions. These six basic emotions are sometimes referred to as **primary** or **universal emotions**. They are anger, fear, surprise, disgust, sadness, and happiness.

All other emotions are described in relation to these primary emotions. Exactly how they relate is explained differently by different theorists.

YOUR TURN

To find out more about the different ways of classifying emotions, go online and search "primary and secondary emotions." Be sure to get permission from a parent, guardian, or teacher before beginning this activity.

DID YOU KNOW?

The study of emotions continues to grow and expand into fields that may surprise you. One of these emerging fields is **neuroeconomics** - quite a mouthful! This area of study is becoming popular with bankers, investors, and money managers. Among other things, it examines how our emotions influence how we invest our money. Knowing that emotions color our experience, we may want to pay attention to our emotions before making any big purchases.

Emotions, Mood, and Temperament

Try This

Let's make three lists together. In the first, make a list of your emotions. In the second, make a list of your feelings. In the third, make a list of your moods. Compare your lists. How many of the same words are on each list?

What's going on?

In everyday language, we often use words like "emotions," "feelings," and "moods" to mean the same thing. But psychologists actually use these terms to express different ideas. Below are Paul Ekman's definitions of these terms.

o **Emotions** are relatively specific and automatic patterns of short-lived physiological and mental responses. They arouse, direct, sustain, and communicate behavior, and help us organize our experiences.

o **Feelings** are more complex experiences. Feelings involve emotions and thoughts about emotions. Jealousy is not an emotion, but a feeling made up of different emotions. When a boyfriend is jealous of losing his girlfriend, he may experience fear, envy or anger. His jealousy may be justified or not. Perhaps it is based on rumors or a misunderstanding. In other classification systems feelings are referred to as **secondary emotions**.

o **Moods** are longer states of feelings and emotions. A mood colors experience. Students in a good mood are more likely to help someone and interpret a teacher's actions as helpful. Students feeling "blue" or depressed are unlikely to take advantage of a teacher's efforts to help with schoolwork.

o **Temperament** is most longstanding. You might want to think of temperament like a **personality trait**. Your temperament makes it likely that you will have a specific emotional reaction to a certain situation. One person may have a sunny disposition and usually sees the bright side of things, even when faced with misfortune: every cloud has a silver lining; to them the glass is always half full. Another person is more cynical and imagines the worst when things go wrong. To these people the glass is always half empty.

o **Emotional Disorders** occur when one emotion dominates a person's life making it difficult for that person to carry out basic tasks, such as eating, sleeping, working, or going to school.

Think of emotions as being grouped in families. A core emotion is at the center with feelings, moods, temperaments, and emotional disorders surrounding this core like ripples in pond. For example, if anger is the core emotion which is rippling away, there will be related feelings such as jealousy or contempt, the mood of being irritable or annoyed, the temperament of being hostile, and emotional disorders involving violence. Rippling away from the primary emotion of sadness are the feelings of remorse or regret, the mood of being "down" or "blue," the temperament of being melancholy, and the emotional disorder of **depression**.

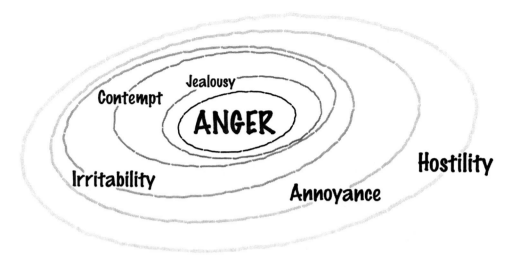

Positive and Negative Emotions

Try This

Conduct a quick poll of friends and family. Try to ask at least ten people the following questions. When you have finished, you can calculate your results into percentages.

1. Do you enjoy watching sad movies?
2. Do you enjoy being frightened by horror movies?
3. Do you enjoy movies that contain "bathroom" humor?

What's Going On?

You should find that some of the people you asked answered yes to one or more of your questions. Perhaps you'll even find that the majority of those polled answered yes. A quick check of the top twenty money-making movies of all time will reveal near the top the movie *Titanic* - a love story with many sad moments. A little further down on the list is the movie *Shrek* - a movie with a fair amount of "bathroom" humor. There is no horror movie in the top twenty, but there are quite a few movies that have frightening, tense scenes such as *Jurassic Park* and *The Lord of the Rings*.

While we often talk about positive and negative emotions, this division may be too simplistic. We usually think of sadness, fear, disgust and anger as negative emotions. But our choice of movies shows that we often enjoy experiencing these emotions. Some people even find pleasure in arguing.

Can you think of an example when amusement, usually considered a positive emotion, is negative? Have you ever been warned by your parent or teacher not to laugh at someone less fortunate than yourself? We typically call this "ridiculing" others, and it's an example of when feeling pleasure is not positive.

Let's remember that one role of emotions is to move us, to motivate us to act. We cannot call fear a negative emotion if it motivates us to run from an approaching gang and, ultimately, keeps us safe. Anger is another emotion that can also lead us to make positive changes. Have you ever found yourself getting angry so that you can get up the courage to confront someone who has been bothering you? If handled properly, your anger might not be considered negative.

What this suggests is that our emotions are complex experiences which are not always easily classified. Emotions do not occur in isolation. Before we can evaluate an emotional response, we must consider what triggered the emotion. Thoughts also play an important part in any emotional experience. In the next chapter we will look more closely at this relationship.

Your Turn

With parental permission, visit the following websites to find out more about the movies that people like to watch: **http://movies.com/boxoffice** and **http://imdb.com**, or go online and word search "box office leaders."

Key Ideas in Chapter 2

Use what you have learned in Chapter 2 to fill in the blanks.

1) When first born, babies display _____.

2) Babies begin to display fear of strangers at _____ months.

3) Most researchers have identified at least _____ primary emotions.

4) Anger can vary in intensity to produce _____ and

_____.

5) The two emotions most similar to joy are _____ and

_____.

6) Fear and surprise combine to produce _____.

7) According to Paul Ekman, emotions are _____-lived.

8) Moods last _____ than emotions.

9) Emotions may either be _____ or

_____.

Keep it in Mind

Using the chart below as your guide, in your notebook write down at least one example of a positive experience and one example of a negative experience for each of the six primary emotions listed. Try to recall and use examples from your own life for this exercise.

Primary Emotion	Positive	Negative
Sadness		
Anger		
Happiness/Pleasure		
Disgust		
Surprise		
Fear		

Answers: 1. general excitement 2. 7-8 months. 3. six. 4. rage and annoyance.
5. anticipation and trust 6. awe. 7. short 8. longer. 9. positive or negative

③ INTERPRETING EMOTIONS

SHOULD I STAY OR SHOULD I GO?

TRY THIS

A popular song of the 1980's asks the question: "Should I stay or should I go?" At the most basic level, our emotions prepare us for one or the other. Imagine yourself in the following scenarios. You have only a split second to decide. Which do you choose?

SCENARIO:	Stay	Go
You notice an unknown stray dog on your lawn. It turns and charges you.	You wait to see if the dog is friendly.	You run for the safety of your house.
You are with your best friend when you see the schoolyard bully in the distance. Your friend owes him money.	You wait with your friend to explain to the bully why you cannot pay him today.	You and your friend slip away and out of sight of the bully for yet another lunch period.
You see a classmate before school. This classmate always asks to copy your homework. You are getting annoyed.	You wait for the classmate to approach you and you tell the classmate, "No."	You try to avoid this classmate. If they do approach you, you let the classmate copy your work, again.
The person you want to ask to the school dance is coming down the hall.	You wait for that person and ask him/her to the dance.	You abruptly turn around and decide it is better to ask at another time.

33

WHAT'S GOING ON?

First, it should be noted that there are no right or wrong answers to the above. Anyone is just as likely to stay as they are to go. Secondly, it should be acknowledged that your answers to the above may not even match what you would actually do if you were suddenly confronted with any of these scenes. In the above activity, you have had the advantage of thinking about these situations. In actuality, the **fight-or-flight response**, as it is commonly called, is so automatic that it can be thought of as the body's **emergency reaction system**.

For example, I had often laughed at stories of people being afraid of mice. When I saw these scenes on TV, I thought they were ridiculously unbelievable. If you had asked me if I would jump on a chair if I saw a mouse in the room, I would have scoffed at the idea. That is what I *thought* I would do. In actuality it was not how I responded when I did suddenly see a mouse dart across my living room floor. Without thinking, I jumped up on the couch shrieking in horror and barely able to call out to my wife. She came into the room and laughed when she saw me, but then she saw the mouse. In no time we were both standing on the couch!

The fight-or-flight response is our emergency reaction when we sense a threat in our environment. A sudden surge of strong emotions can activate this system. While we will spend most of this chapter examining the relationship between thoughts and emotion, this is one instance where we clearly react before we have a chance to think. From a survival standpoint, there seems to be advantages to having such a system. If our prehistoric ancestors were suddenly confronted with a charging sabertooth tiger, it is advantageous to act first and think later. If you are suddenly confronted with a speeding car, an emergency reaction to jump out of the way could save your life.

The Science

When the emergency reaction system is activated, the amygdala orders the body to release a set of chemicals. These are usually called **stress chemicals**. They are made in two areas in your body called **adrenal glands**, one just above each kidney in your lower back. The adrenal glands produce a number of chemicals known as **hormones**. These are essential in helping you to survive dangerous situations.

Three important chemicals are **cortisol, adrenaline** or **norepinephrine**, and **fibrogen**.

Cortisol's main job is to increase the amount of sugar - **glucose** - that you have in your blood by chemically breaking down proteins and fats. Cortisol raises your blood pressure. It does this so that your muscles can quickly have extra fuel for movement. It also delays the effects of damage to muscles, which will bruise up and become stiff and painful if you've had to run or fight your way out of trouble.

Another important chemical made in the adrenal gland is adrenaline or norepinephrine. Adrenaline's main job is to make you more alert and to speed up your reactions. It works together with cortisol by increasing the heart rate and the force that the heart uses to pump the blood out. Adrenaline also helps to release energy by converting the body's store of sugar - called **glycogen** - into glucose. It widens the tubes in the lungs to make breathing easier. It also directs blood away from your internal organs and digestive system so that more is available for the arms and legs to stay and fight or to escape.

Lastly, **fibrogen** enters the blood stream to help to heal any cuts you might get as you are escaping or fighting. It does this by thickening the blood so that it will clot faster.

WHEN THE FIGHT OR FLIGHT EMERGENCY REACTION SYSTEM IS ACTIVATED:

1) The rate and strength of the heartbeat increases, allowing oxygen to be pumped more rapidly which helps keep us awake and alert.

2) The spleen contracts and releases stored red blood cells to carry the extra oxygen.

3) The liver releases stored sugar to provide energy to muscles.

4) The blood supply is redistributed away from the skin and to the muscles and brain.

5) Respiration deepens.

6) The pupils widen, to let more light in to see better.

7) The blood's ability to seal wounds is increased.
(Gray, 1984)

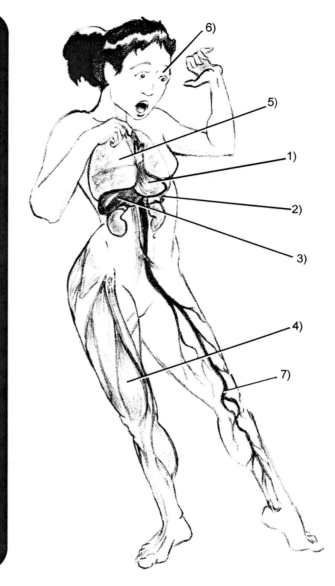

The **involuntary response** activated by emotions is only part of our emotional experience. If it weren't, I might still be up on the couch in flight from a mouse.

Appraising the Situation ("Emotional Cycle")

Try This

Try to remember two different emotional incidents from your life: in the first episode where your emotional response was appropriate for the situation; in the second incident where you now realize your emotional response was inappropriate. Write down the details of both incidents. Try to remember what triggered your emotions, which emotions you experienced, and how you reacted. For the second incident, try to remember why your response was inappropriate. Did you overreact? Did your reaction make the situation worse?

What's going on?

Our emotional responses involve an appraisal of the situation. An appraisal is our understanding of the meaning of the event. Appraising the situation involves evaluating it. In the split seconds that we are confronted with a situation, we seek to determine whether or not something is good or bad, helpful or hurtful; whether we are being confronted by something that is strong or weak, fast or slow; and whether are we being confronted by something that is active.

Our initial appraisal will lead to a certain action (or inaction). We then receive feedback to help us determine what to do next. This leads to a reappraisal and more feedback - a continuation of the first action or a change of course. Almost every situation is complex enough to require continuous appraisal.

Consider the situation in which I was confronted by a mouse in my apartment. Seeing the mouse triggered an initial appraisal: hurtful, fast, and active, so I jumped out of the way. Once safe, I was able to reappraise the situation, and I drew some new conclusions: the threat turned out to be weak, still fast, but not actively attacking. It actually was moving quickly away from me, no doubt after going through its own appraisal process! Something about a hundred times larger was moving toward *it*! In the end, I was able to trap the mouse safely and remove it from the apartment.

Initial appraisals are often not conscious, so some researchers refer to them as **automatic appraisals** or **autoappraisals**. These appraisals can be innate (we are born with them), such as fear of snakes. Other appraisals are learned, such as getting angry when we are driving on the freeway and a car gets too close.

Our emotional response is not an isolated event. It is part of a cycle. The cycle involves **a trigger, primary appraisal, an emotion, a reaction, feedback of that information, continuous reappraisals, and more feedback from the reappraisals**. Our feelings change as new information comes in. In my situation with the mouse, I remember feeling multiple feelings from my initial fear to embarrassment for jumping onto a couch, to anger at having my evening rudely interrupted.

Sometimes when appraising a situation, we make mistakes. I would say that I overreacted when I saw the mouse. Review the situations you wrote about in the activity above. Can you pinpoint any mistakes you made in appraising the situation which led to your inappropriate emotional response?

Try This

Here are two alternative activities. You can do them both if you like, or choose the one that you can most easily relate to.

A. Think about a time when you were interacting with an angry adult. The adult was accusing you of some misdeed, but you knew you were innocent. You tried to convince the adult, but all your attempts failed. In fact, the adult seemed to get even angrier and accuse you of other things. Write about this incident. Describe it in as much detail as you can. Recreate the dialogue. Consider the appraisals and reappraisals involved. Also, consider any other emotions that may have emerged.

B. Think about a time when you observed someone who seemed too afraid of something. Maybe you or a friend did not want to ride a particular roller coaster although you went on all the other rides. Maybe you or a friend did not want to approach a boy or girl to talk because of a secret "crush." Maybe you know someone who is afraid of dogs or won't eat a particular type of food because s/he finds it disgusting. Write about what you observed. Write about what people said to them or may have said to help them overcome their fear.

WHAT'S GOING ON?

In Chapter 1, you learned that emotions help organize our experience, that is, they "color" our experiences. The above activities tried to demonstrate this. In particular, emotions color how we appraise and reappraise a situation.

This explains why it can be difficult for an angry person to hear your side of the story. An angry person is likely to interpret what you are saying to support his/her angry response. Our brains are organized not to challenge why we are having a particular emotion, but to support it. Under these circumstances an attempt to convince an angry person of your innocence might easily be appraised as an attempt to make excuses or be deceptive. When a hostile person looks out on the world, they see a hostile world full of potential threats.

If a person is afraid to look out of the window of a tall building, you cannot always reason with them that it is safe. The fear they experience does not allow for that immediate reappraisal.

In life-threatening situations we can appreciate the brain's working this way. We remain focused on the task at hand, and the emotions direct and sustain appropriate actions. However, many of our emotional responses do not occur under dire circumstances, and an awareness of the bias in the reappraisal of the emotional process can help us to avoid inappropriate emotional responses.

The Past is Present

Try This

Ask a friend to recall a recent incident that provoked an emotional response. Then ask them to associate this incident with a similar incident from their past. See how far back in time you can lead them. Can they recall a similar incident from 6 months ago? One year ago? Two years ago?

What's Going On?

We remember past events as well as the accompanying emotions. When confronted with a similar event in the present, we will often respond to the present event with the same emotions that we had with the past event. For example, if a child has often experienced being criticized, he will respond with similar feelings when criticized by a teacher. If his response to the parent was to feel hurt and withdraw, he may feel hurt in class and refuse to participate. If his response to the parent was to feel hurt, angry, and yell, he will probably get angry and become argumentative in class.

Sometimes we may react strongly to similar events. At other times, we may only have a weak reaction. We may not even understand or realize why we are suddenly feeling a little uneasy, hurt or angry.

From a survival standpoint, there are advantages to recognizing similar events from our past and reacting accordingly. Our emotions are activated to promote quick reactions that could save our lives. However, as we grow older, reactions that were helpful as a child may prove to cause more problems as a teenager. Reacting to constructive criticism from a teacher in the same way that you may have responded to an overly critical parent could cause more problems at school and prevent you from learning an important lesson.

Perhaps you had an older sibling who would tease you to get you angry. Your older sibling almost always continued to tease you until you became so angry that you started trying to hit her. You may encounter similar teasing at school. Your initial appraisal of the situation will probably stir up the emotions you have felt with your older sibling. At school, it would only cause more problems to react like you did with your sibling and try to hit the person teasing you. Your emotional reaction may even prevent you from noticing that the person at school was not trying to be mean, but awkwardly trying to express friendship.

Your Turn

Think about some recent misunderstandings you have observed between people you know at school. Consider whether or not the situation may have been complicated by one person who was appraising and responding to the present event as if it were the same as a past event. Perhaps you can even think of an incident in which you were involved.

Thoughts and Emotions

Try This

Write about a time when you may have been in class (or another place) and you thought someone was talking about you. Try to describe this incident completely. What led up to it? Were you alone or with someone else? How did you react? Did you react immediately or did your emotional response build slowly? What was the outcome?

What's Going On?

While there are many instances when our emotional response comes before our thoughts, there are times when our thoughts trigger emotions. Consider the above example. Our emotional reaction is likely to depend on what we think the other person is saying about us. If we think they are being negative, we could become angry; on the other hand, if we think they are saying nice things about us, we are likely to feel good. Unlike our fight-or-flight response, this is a slower route to an emotional response.

Feelings like fear of tomorrow's test often follow this slower route. Our fear or apprehension grows as we think and talk about the test with our friends. Embarrassment is another feeling that follows this slower route.

YOUR TURN

Recall a time when your thoughts preceded a specific emotional response. Did you feel like someone was disrespecting you or cheating you? Or, perhaps you did something that received unexpected praise.

AMBIGUOUS SITUATIONS

TRY THIS

Review the following first-person account with friends or relatives. Try to guess what the author was feeling.

A few years ago, I flew to Los Angeles to give a lecture. I enjoy lecturing and was looking forward to the meeting. I was listening to the speaker who preceded me, waiting for my turn, when a most bizarre thing happened. I began to feel shaky...When I noticed this, I began to berate myself, silently: "I should have prepared more. I should have written out my speech. Why didn't I fly in last night and get a good night's sleep before the talk?" And there were more...ideas about what I should have done.

WHAT'S GOING ON?

Before continuing, read the rest of this account.

What was surprising was that I had never felt like this before in my life. I lecture often on subjects I know well, and I was prepared. But was I nervous! Then it began to dawn on me, slowly. I truly felt "shaky." My arms were shaking, so was my hand. Then I looked around. The table was shaking, the glasses on it almost spilled their water. The podium was shaking... As soon as I saw what was actually happening, I wasn't nervous anymore.

(Ornstein, op. cit., p. 411)

The author was not shaking because he was nervous; he was experiencing an earthquake! What this example illustrates is that our brains interpret our internal states and assign an emotion to how we are feeling. Feeling shaky is a common physical response to being nervous, so the author's primary appraisal was nervousness. How do you think he reappraised the situation? What emotions may have accompanied the new understanding of being in an earthquake?

The above situation doesn't happen every day; more common is confusion that arises in a situation because the internal states or feelings of many different emotions are similar. Changes in our heartbeat and breathing, feelings in our digestive tract, stomach, or gut are a few of the more obvious similarities. Because of these similarities in our reactions to **ambiguous (uncertain) situations**, we are not always sure which emotion we are having. Consider these experiments.

While listening to their own heartbeats, women were shown slides of people who had experienced violent death. However, they were not actually hearing their own heartbeat, but a recording. During some of the slides, the heart rate was increased. The slides that were shown while the women heard the increased heartbeat were rated as significantly more unpleasant and discomforting.

In another experiment, men were shown pictures of women and told that they were listening to their own heartbeat. Of course, again, it was a recording. Five out of the ten slides were accompanied by an increased heart rate. Can you guess which women were rated more attractive? The photos accompanied by the rapid heartbeat were rated more attractive.

A series of studies conducted in the 1970s demonstrates that misinterpreting our internal state can lead us to finding other people more attractive. In a 1974 experiment, a woman interviews two groups of men. The men are interviewed individually. One group of men is interviewed on a stable, solid bridge. The other group is interviewed on a wobbly, swaying bridge. The experimenters wanted to find out whether the emotional arousal caused by being in a dangerous situation would lead men to find the woman more attractive.

At the end of the interview, each man interviewed was given the phone number of the woman and told they could phone back for more information on the experiment. The experimenters reasoned that if they found the woman attractive, they would be more likely to call back. The men interviewed on the wobbly bridge were more than four times likely to call back! The experiment showed that 50 percent of the men from the wobbly bridge called compared to 12.5 percent from the stable bridge. The internal state aroused by crossing a wobbly bridge was misinterpreted as feeling attraction.

Other studies revealed similar results. One study showed that exercising with a member of the opposite sex could be provocative. It's true in real life that more people will get married during disasters and wartime than they do in peace-time. Did you ever wonder why activities such as going to an amusement park or to a scary horror movie were so popular with dates?

In ambiguous situations, we are more likely to misinterpret our emotional reactions. However, most situations are not ambiguous, and, therefore, our emotions are usually an accurate and immediate guide for us.

KEY IDEAS IN CHAPTER 3

For the following questions answer A) True or B) False.

1. The fight-or-flight response is an emergency activation system.
   A) True   B) False

2. The amygdala plays an important role in the fight-or-flight response.
   A) True   B) False

3. An appraisal is our understanding of the meaning of an event.
   A) True   B) False

4. All appraisals are final and reappraisals are not necessary.
   A) True   B) False

5. An emotional response is an isolated event.
   A) True   B) False

6. Our feelings change as new information is processed.
   A) True   B) False

7. Our emotions can color how we appraise a situation.
   A) True   B) False

8. Internal states of different emotions may be similar.
   A) True   B) False

9. People don't misinterpret feeling attracted to another in a dangerous situation.
   A) True   B) False

10. Our emotions are usually reliable guides.
    A) True   B) False

Answers: 1.A 2.A 3.A 4.B 5.B 6.A 7.A 8.A 9.B 10.A

KEEP IT IN MIND

Continue with your "Emotions Log." As you describe each event, try to identify the different components of the emotional cycle. What triggered the response? What emotions (or emotion) were aroused? What was your primary appraisal? Did you reappraise the situation? Remember, emotional responses often occur in seconds. Often we do not become aware of actively appraising a situation until after we have acted. A daily log can help you begin to become more aware of your responses. Here is a sample:

"Today I felt a variety of emotions. I was worried about what I was going to write about. I didn't feel any strong emotion today. I was too worried about what I was going to write that I didn't know I was feeling worried and pressured. What triggered my worry was school had ended and I hadn't felt a strong emotion. Then I remembered that I felt a little frustrated during math. I could write about this. In math my group was stuck and didn't know how to solve a problem but it wasn't that frustrating because we just asked the teacher. Maybe I should write about how I felt a little envy when I heard some people talking about an Xbox 360. I want one but my dad won't buy it. I'll show him. I am going to save up the money and buy it myself. Just right now I'm feeling annoyed at mom because she's trying to help me. Over and over I have to say I don't want your help and she accuses me of being disrespectful."

- Caleb

4 ANGER

"In P.E. we played baseball. We played another class and we creamed them. But the thing that made me angry was the captain of the other team kept on cussing at the people who weren't good at baseball. I don't know why some guys get so angry. This kid was just yelling at people. It was just plain mean. Why get so worked up? Like baseball is going to be your professional career? I don't think so!"

- Lauren

Facial Expressions

Try This

Examine these pictures. The one on the left is a neutral expression. The one on the right shows anger. Write down the distinguishing characteristics of an angry facial expression.

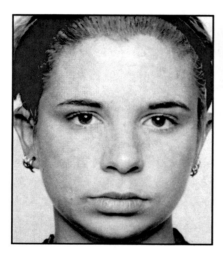 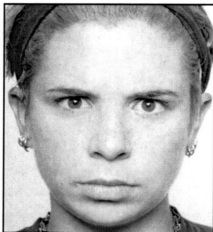

What's Going On?

Anger is a primary emotion, and the facial expression for anger is the same all over the world.

o The eyebrows lower and draw together, causing vertical lines to appear above the nose.
o The eyes have a hard stare and may bulge out.
o The lips are pressed together or open into a squarish shape as in shouting.

Your Turn

Look in the mirror and make an angry face. Now, notice the characteristics as described above. Pay attention to what this face feels like. It is very difficult, some would say impossible, to suppress this face when feeling angry, even if we only "flash" it for a microsecond. If you become more familiar with what an emotional facial expression feels like, you will more consciously be able to identify when you are angry.

Nonverbal Expressions

Try This

Ask some friends or relatives to strike an angry pose. Remind them that they can't speak. They can only use nonverbal gestures. Note the different ways people express anger.

What's Going On?

While our facial expression for anger is universal, many of our other expressions are learned and are culturally based. In different parts of the world, people will show that they are angry in different ways. Tourists are often warned to be careful with their hand gestures when visiting other countries: the sign for OK in the United States (thumbs up or circle with thumb and forefinger) is an angry, insulting gesture in some other countries.

Some common display signals when angry are clenched fists or clawed hands. People may raise their arms as if to strike a punch. Sometimes people will lean toward you in an aggressive manner.

Your Turn

With parent or guardian permission, image search the word "anger" on the internet. Write down a description of the different nonverbal display signals of anger.

Did You Know?

Nonverbal gestures of all sorts vary from country to country. Consider the gesture of pointing. In the United States, people point with the index finger. In Germany people use the little finger. In Japan people use the whole hand; pointing with the index finger is considered rude! When counting on our fingers, people in the U.S. start with the index finger as number one. In Germany people count the thumb as number one. In Indonesia the middle finger is number one.

http://www.andrews.edu/~tidwell/lead689/NonVerbal.html

Verbal Expression

Try This

Make a list of some common things you say to someone to indicate that you are angry. Repeat one or two of these expressions in an angry tone and then in a neutral tone. Note the distinguishing characteristics of an angry tone of voice.

What's Going On?

Verbal expressions of emotion are not universal. They vary from culture to culture although similarities may exist. As with non-verbal expressions, different cultures have rules about socially acceptable ways of expressing anger. These are called **display rules**. While it is socially acceptable to be loud and expressive in many southern European cultures, in many East Asian cultures the same behavior is socially unacceptable.

In the United States, when angry, people often use profanity to express themselves. People also raise the volume of their voices and speak more rapidly. Sometimes it sounds as if people are forcing the words out at you - sort of hitting you with their words.

Your Turn

Watch for scenes where anger is displayed in movies or on TV. Make notes on the various displays: facial, nonverbal, and verbal.

The Anger Continuum

Try This

Make a list of words that mean anger. Try to find at least ten words that mean anger. If you are having trouble getting started, check out a thesaurus or dictionary.

Indignation
Fury
Wrath
Resentment
Rage
Ire

WHAT'S GOING ON?

Anger varies in intensity from annoyance to rage. We use different words to indicate just how angry we may be feeling. If we are slightly angry, we say we are annoyed. If we are very angry, we may say we are outraged, or furious, or just really mad. Hatred can be considered an extreme form of anger.

Anger varies in duration. We talk about moods when we are feeling angry for a longer period of time. If we are feeling mildly angry for a longer period, we say we are feeling irritable. If we are very angry for a longer period, we may be in a hostile mood.

Frustration often results in anger. We can become frustrated with another person or an inanimate object.

Violence is a more extreme action resulting from being angry. Hitting is quite common in younger children, especially toddlers. Parents train their children not to hit others, and most children learn to express their anger in more socially appropriate ways. The recent rise in school violence is an indication that the adults of society are not paying enough attention to helping youngsters deal more effectively with their emotions. When violence continues into adulthood, it is seen as a sign of an emotional disorder that can lead to criminal behavior.

EMOTIONS CAN BLEND WITH OTHER EMOTIONS.

Anger can blend with disgust. When breaking up with a boyfriend or girlfriend, we often find ourselves feeling sad and angry. Whether these emotions actually blend together or rapidly shift back and forth is a question researchers are investigating. In all likelihood, it is both. If confronted by a hostile animal or person, we may shift from being afraid to being angry several times.

Your Turn

Go through old magazines and newspapers and look for photos of angry people. Try to identify the different levels of anger. Perhaps you will find some blends that you may not be able to identify totally. Put them aside until we explore the distinguishing facial expressions of other emotions in later chapters. Other types of anger include: fury, resentment, exasperation, indignation, animosity, and wrath.

Getting Angry

Try This

Make a list of things that get you angry. Ask a friend or relative to make a list. Compare your lists. Can you add to your list after comparing? How many things did you have in common? Were you surprised by some of the things that made your friend or relative angry?

What's Going On?

Why people become angry:

1. We become angry when someone interferes with what we want to do. If we think that the interference is on purpose, our anger may be stronger. Frustration is a type of interference with our goals which is why it often results in anger.

2. We become angry when someone is trying to hurt us. The hurt can be physical or psychological; someone could be trying to hit us or insult us. When others get angry with us, we usually feel "attacked" and respond by becoming angry, too.

3. We become angry when someone we care about has disappointed us.

4. We become angry when someone rejects us.

5. We become angry when someone suggests an action or belief that we find offensive.

Like all emotions, anger is complex. Some may respond more intensely to some situations and less to others. Sometimes our anger may direct us to stand up for ourselves and other times we may decide it is best to withdraw from the situation. Our anger is useful to defend ourselves.

When we find that we are angry, we should take the time to figure out why we have become angry because this anger signals that something needs to change. We can't make effective change unless we know the source of our anger.

Our anger is also a way to signal to someone else that we need some space. Our anger warns others to back off or stop doing whatever they are doing.

However, sometimes anger can become a problem especially if it leads us to hurt other people unnecessarily. Remember that emotions color our experiences and interpretations. Once an event has triggered our anger, we are likely to continue to reappraise the situation to justify being angry. For example, if I become angry at a driver on the freeway for cutting me off, I am less likely to consider that it was accidental. I might consider it deliberate and plan to defend myself by attacking back. You can see how quickly this incident can spiral out of control and lead to **road rage**. If I drive up next to the other driver and begin shouting out my window, how do you expect he will act?

On the other hand, if you consider the millions of cars on the road daily and the thousands of times people are cut off, road rage is a rare event. You realize that anger, like all emotions, can be managed effectively most of the time.

While most of the time we are able to benefit from its useful call to action without suffering from its destructive side, there are those times when we wished we had done something differently.

Did You Know?

Research has confirmed what parents have known for years. Lack of sleep can increase feelings of irritability. Sleep deprivation has a negative effect on all people, not just children. It isn't just irritability that increases, but all emotional responses seem to be heightened, whereas our ability to make logical decisions seems to be impaired.

Recent research has revised the recommendation of eight hours of sleep. It is now recommended that teens get at least 9 hours and 15 minutes sleep per night to function at their best.

Your Turn

Watch a sporting event live or on TV. Notice how often you see flashes of anger across a player's face. How can anger be helpful to an athlete during a sporting event?

Managing Anger

Try This

Think of something that has made you angry. Take note of how your body feels and what nonverbal gestures you use. Especially notice the universal facial expression for being angry. To help you get angry, think about an incident in your past that really got you mad. Replay that incident until you feel angry again and can notice how it feels. Review the distinguishing characteristics of the facial expression described at the start of the chapter.

WHAT'S GOING ON?

Often we become angry without even realizing it. If you want to manage your anger, it is helpful to recognize how you feel when you are angry. Pay particular attention to how your face feels. Some of your internal feelings may be ambiguous, in other words, similar to other emotions, but the facial expression for anger is unique and universal.

Become familiar with how your face feels when you are angry. Keep in mind that this expression may only last for seconds. But for most of us, the face doesn't lie. The first step in learning to manage your anger is realizing that you are angry as soon as possible. With this understanding, you can begin to make more effective reappraisals of your situation.

TRY THIS

Review the list you created in the previous activity of things that get you angry. Create a new list by ranking these anger triggers in order from those that provoke the most intense angry response to those that provoke a mild response. Add to the list if you can. You may find it helpful to look over the general reasons that people get angry to see what situations might apply that you had not considered. Remember, getting angry includes everything from annoyance to outrage.

WHAT'S GOING ON?

It is unrealistic never to expect to get angry. Often we get angry and react before we are even consciously aware we are angry. Biologically this makes sense. Our emotions have evolved to keep us safe. They are supposed to provoke immediate action. With this in mind, if we need or want to manage our anger more effectively, we will find it difficult to suppress or stuff our anger.

More realistic is to identify those situations or actions that trigger our anger. Identifying our anger triggers, especially those which lead us to overreact, can help us to make more effective reappraisals when we find ourselves feeling angry. For example, there was a time I would become very angry when other drivers cut me off. It became so bad that my wife and son were stressed to drive with me because I was likely to respond very foolishly - getting angry and chasing other drivers down the freeway only seemed to escalate angry feelings and wasn't very effective. After one particular frightening incident that got out of hand, I realized that I needed to manage these angry outbursts. I began by identifying the trigger for these outbursts: other vehicles driving recklessly. This hasn't stopped me from becoming angry with reckless drivers, but I have learned to recognize why I have become angry and reappraise the situation so that I can take more effective action. I can reappraise the situation as not being a threat or a willful effort to hurt me. With this reappraisal, I have been able to manage my response and avoid road rage.

Did You Know?

People who are often angry or aggressive are at a higher risk of developing life-threatening illnesses than less hostile people. Heart disease is a major risk for angry people. Angry people also seem to be more likely to engage in other unhealthy, risky behavior such as overeating, excessive drinking, and smoking. Angry people tend to have fewer friends which means they don't benefit as much from the positive effects of social contact. Friendships can provide us with support that reduces stress, which is good for the heart.

Hostility in teenagers has been linked to obesity, high blood pressure, and the onset of type II diabetes. These conditions are associated with increased risk of heart disease as an adult.

Try This

Read the following scenario about a girl who did not effectively handle her anger. Then rewrite the scenario with alternative endings that show more effective ways to manage anger.

Tanya has a weekend job at a crafts store. Her supervisor, Miss Spears, tells her to clean a spill on aisle 5. Tanya feels as if Miss Spears always gives her the "dirty" jobs while her coworker, Brittany, never gets asked to clean spills. Tanya tells Miss Spears, "Ask Brittany. I'm busy and still have to stock the shelves in aisle 8 before leaving in an hour." Miss Spears snaps, "Stop making excuses. Please clean aisle 5." When Miss Spears turns around, Tanya "gives her the finger" and mutters, "Bitch." Miss Spears hears Tanya and sends her home immediately. She informs Tanya that she'll be getting a call from the store manager tomorrow to discuss her future with the company.

One strategy for managing emotional outbursts is to rehearse those scenes that trigger an emotional response. One common strategy for expressing feelings is to make "I" statements. An alternative for Tanya could be, "I am not making excuses. I feel angry when you say that. I am stressing to finish aisle 8 before going home."

If you know that you are going into a situation that usually gets you angry, imagine the scene and appropriate ways of responding. Try writing down these alternatives if you can. If you have already had an angry outburst, write about it in your journal. In your journal write down alternatives - what you wished you had said or done. You can't stop yourself from getting angry, but in most cases you can learn to handle your anger the way you want to.

The Science

Most animals have to fight to survive. Being aggressive is a day-to-day fact of life. Animals have to fight or run to catch food or to avoid being eaten by something else. Anger motivates an animal to fight off a predator or another animal who might want a share of the catch.

Aggression also plays a part in the way some creatures reproduce. For instance, male deer will fight each other for the right to choose their mate as a way of making sure that the strongest genes are passed on to the next generation. Mothers will fight ferociously to defend their young from predators. Most of us have heard the saying, "Never get between a mother and her cub!"

Human beings are no different. We defend our loved ones, possessions and ourselves. We also become angry when defending our status and self esteem. Many young men end up in prison having assaulted someone else for treating them with "disrespect." Anger will also well up when we feel that our beliefs and values are under attack, and we're even capable of killing and risking death to defend these beliefs.

Some people enjoy the angry feeling because it makes them feel strong and in control, yet others are keen to get rid of the feeling as soon as they can. However, the brains of people who have an aggressive temperament are slightly different than non-aggressive people. There seems to be less brain activity in the **prefrontal cortex** of the **frontal lobes**. This is the part of the brain where we think things through and put the brakes on angry impulses. People with chronic aggression do not so much have an anger problem as a lack of a thinking-twice-before-lashing-out problem.

This can be caused by a lot of things: head injuries, certain diseases, alcohol, and drug abuse. It has also been found that very high or very low levels of **serotonin** in the brain can also lead to overaggressiveness. In an angry person the amygdala send signals to the prefrontal cortex. The blood flow increases to the prefrontal cortex and decreases to amygdala. At this point our brain is primed to reappraise the situation and moderate our behavior. Recent studies show that in people who are overaggressive, the blood flow does not increase to the prefrontal cortex. Instead, blood flow decreases to the prefrontal cortex and increases to the amygdala. This keeps people in "fight" mode and accounts for the continued aggression.

All of us can have problems in reappraisal. In deciding how to act, the prefrontal cortex searches for appropriate memories or learned behaviors. Problems occur when the learned behavior recalled from a similar situation isn't exactly appropriate. For example, if you had an older brother who always teased you for making mistakes on your school work, you might react to a teacher correcting you in the same way. Before you realize it, you may get angry and argumentative in class. You are defending yourself like you did against your brother. Unfortunately, your teacher is not your brother and constructive criticism is not the same as teasing.

The good news is that *learned behavior can be relearned*. Although, it takes a much greater effort to relearn how to react to a certain stimulus than the initial reaction took to learn.

Key Ideas in Chapter 4

Copy the outline of the head on the following page into your notebook. Sketch in the key features of an angry facial expression. Label these distinguishing characteristics.

Keep it in Mind

As you become better at recognizing anger in yourself, you may find that you are better at recognizing it in others, too. Be careful about pointing out when others are angry. Recognizing what emotions others are feeling doesn't tell us why they are feeling that way. We might recognize the emotion, but we may not really know the source. For example, at school don't jump to the conclusion that your friend is angry at you or something that is happening in class. They may be thinking about an argument they had at home.

Also, others may not want to share their feelings with you and may even be embarrassed to find out that their face gave them away. If you notice someone is angry and you want to do something, change the way you behave toward that person. Remember emotions color experience. Make sure your approach cannot be misunderstood as aggressive.

If you are very close to the person and decide to try and talk, take an approach that gives the person the option not to talk. You might say something like, "You seem to be angry. Would you like to talk about it?" If they deny being angry, don't insist - even if their facial expression reveals otherwise. Sometimes a person needs a little space or a little more time to reappraise their emotions.

5 FEAR

"After school I called my friend Chris. I was worried because he had been acting weird and I just wanted to know what's up. I talked to him and told him that I wasn't sure we were still friends because we went from talking all the time and eating lunch together to never talking and seeing each other. He agreed, but said it wasn't because he didn't want to be friends. He told me he definitely still wanted to be friends. I felt relieved. We agreed to talk more and have lunch together tomorrow."

- Lauren

EXPRESSIONS OF FEAR

TRY THIS

Examine the following pictures. The one on the left is a neutral facial expression; the one on the right shows fear. Write down the distinguishing characteristics of the facial expression of fear.

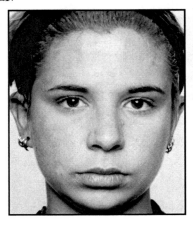 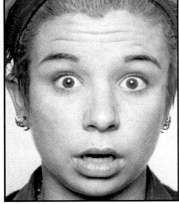

WHAT'S GOING ON?

Fear is a primary emotion and the facial expression for fear is recognized around the world. The distinguishing characteristics are:

o The eyebrows raise and draw together.

o The forehead wrinkles in the center but not at the sides.

o The upper and lower eyelids raise.

o The mouth opens and the lips tense slightly.

This universal facial expression serves to warn others that a threat is nearby. By signaling fear, we alert others to help us or run for safety. Sometimes looking fearful or worried causes others to be merciful. Have you ever noticed an angry teacher at school suddenly calm down when they observe that the student becomes fearful or worried? Perhaps you have been involved in this type of situation? Some children learn to manipulate their parents by pretending to be afraid or worried. However, sometimes looking afraid encourages an attacker to continue. The attacker may be looking for easy prey and a fearful facial expression indicates a willingness to back down or not fight back. This is one reason schoolyard fights often include a lot of posturing. Students may not want to fight, but they also do not want to appear afraid. In this case they will dance around each other until an adult arrives on the scene to break it up.

Look in the mirror and try to reproduce this face. Become familiar with what fear in your face feels like. When fear, or any emotion, "flashes" for just a second, it is called a **micro-expression**. As you become more familiar with what this emotion feels like, you can better identify when you are afraid.

Your Turn

Look through newspapers and magazines for photos showing people that are afraid. Create a scrapbook. Identify other nonverbal expressions of fear. What do people do with their hands? How do they hold their bodies? While the facial expression for fear is universal, other nonverbal gestures may be culturally specific - unique to a certain group of people.

More Fun

With your parent's permission, watch some movies where people are afraid. Are there any distinguishing verbal characteristics? Horror movies from various countries can be found in most video rental stores. Compare and contrast how people react fearfully in these presentations.

Becoming Afraid

Try This

Talk to friends and relatives about what makes people afraid and make a list of what you and they think of.

What's going on?

Fear is the result of a perceived threat, which can be physical or psychological, real or imaginary. We can learn to fear anything, but there are some unlearned triggers of fear. The sudden loss of physical support, so that we feel like we are falling through space, provokes fear. This can happen if we miss a step or, if you have ever traveled by airplane, when the plane suddenly loses altitude. There is a fear of physical pain: most adults still cringe before getting a shot at the doctor's office despite having received many. We fear something hurling through space quickly in our direction. A harmless paper wad will cause someone to duck or react if seen from the corner of the eye.

PING!

Most people have to work hard not to react when something harmless is thrown at them even if they know it is harmless. Snakes may be another unlearned trigger although some people seem not to be afraid of them.

Anything that seems to be a threat can be feared. Children often become afraid for no apparent reason. It takes a patient and compassionate parent or adult to reassure a person who is afraid. Reasoning or dismissing another's fear is often not effective. As with any emotion, it may take time before a person can reappraise the cause of their fear.

There are two different fearful actions: freezing/hiding or fleeing. Which we choose often depends on what we have learned in the past about the action which is most likely to protect us. Animals will freeze in headlights in an attempt to hide from an approaching "creature." Have you ever played the game "Hide and Seek"? Most children stay hidden and still until it becomes obvious that they are seen, then they will flee. The fact that fleeing is a favored response might explain why many teenagers run if they believe they are going to get in trouble even if they know that they stand to get in less trouble by staying and accepting responsibility. It also explains why running away from home often occurs after a child has received a bad report card.

Another common reaction when afraid is to become angry. We will often experience these two emotions in quick succession. Which emotion comes first or dominates any situation will depend upon the individual and the threat. This could explain whether you choose to fight or take flight.

The Science

Experiments have demonstrated the body's adaptations to fleeing in the face of danger. When faced with danger, our bodies automatically surge blood to the large muscles in the legs. This blood surge prepares these muscles to work harder and longer.

The Fear Continuum

Try This

Review the list you created in the above activity or create a new list of things that cause you to be afraid. Divide the list into two categories: immediate threats and not immediate threats.

What's Going On?

Our behavior differs whether or not we appraise a threat as immediate or not immediate (impending).

A. An immediate threat leads to freezing or fleeing as an action to deal with the threat, while an impending threat leads to increased alertness for danger, vigilance, and muscular tension.

B. The response to an immediate threat leads to a reduction in pain sensation, an adaptation that allows us to continue to act - fight-or-flight response. The response to an impending threat magnifies pain, an adaptation that draws our attention to the fact that something is wrong and we need to pay attention to it.

C. Our brain activity differs whether we perceive the threat as immediate or not immediate.

Try This

Make a list of all the words that mean fear. If you need help, ask friends or relatives.

What's Going On?

Like all emotions, fear varies. We have already discussed that fear varies whether or not we see the threat as immediate or impending. Fear also varies in intensity. We may be mildly fearful or apprehensive to extremely fearful or terrified.

Also fear varies in duration. An anxious person is someone who remains vigilant for an impending threat for a long time. **Shyness** is a type of fearfulness experienced for longer periods.

You don't have to be on the edge of panic to feel worry and **anxiety**, which are very different. Worry happens when our minds focus and dwell upon scary things that are actually happening in our lives; but anxiety happens when we are afraid of something that might happen (but isn't actually happening at the moment). These two things are very similar to each other and often happen at the same time.

Anxiety is always a problem because the mind is making unhelpful connections between scary memories and non-threatening objects or situations. This can sometimes take an extreme form called a **panic attack**. This happens when the amygdala makes an inaccurate match between something in the world outside to a scary memory and sets off the fight-or-flight response. The person may not have any idea what caused their brain to do this, and the rising feeling of panic can become extremely scary in itself. The panic then "feeds off" itself. A panic attack can begin when someone is feeling generally stressed, and the amygdala is already close to the edge of fight-or-flight response. What makes a panic attack different from other anxiety problems is the speed with which it happens and the intensity of the feelings once they're switched on.

Most emotional disorders connected with fear are usually the result of people continually perceiving threats in the environment when there are none.

Did You Know?

Repeated attacks of anxiety indicate a lot of stress. High levels of stress have been linked to many health problems because stress lowers our **immune system** - our ability to fight off diseases. While high levels of stress have been linked to increased risk of heart attacks and the spread of cancer, it also contributes to the increase in those everyday health concerns of colds, the flu, and herpes. Gastrointestinal problems, or "stomach aches," have also been associated with high levels of stress.

The Science

The brain is made up of billions of cells called **neurons**. These neurons "talk" to each other by sending electrical pulses from one to another. This is the way the brain does all the work of its thinking, remembering, and feeling. But the ends of these neuron cells don't quite meet each other. When an electrical signal reaches the end of one neuron, it somehow has to get the message it was carrying to jump the gap to the next neuron. It does this by causing a chemical called a **neurotransmitter** to cross the space to the next neuron. Different neurotransmitters carry different types of messages across the gap.

Some people are more prone to feeling anxious than others. Researchers have found that people are born with brains that make more or less of the neurotransmitter **serotonin**. Serotonin's job is to stop the brain from worrying too much by calming us down and helping us to realize we are okay. Serotonin helps us to feel positive and good about ourselves. The less serotonin you have in your brain, the more likely you are to feel anxious.

Did You Know?

"**Phobia**" is the Greek word for "fear." It refers to an extreme or unfounded fear of a specific object or place. The most common phobias are **zoophobia** or fear of animals, **claustrophobia** or fear of closed spaces, and **acrophobia** or fear of heights. Other phobias include **agoraphobia** or the fear of being in open or public places, and school phobia, the fear of going to school.

A "modern" phobia is **aviophobia** or fear of flying. A 2006 poll indicates that 9% of all Americans are very afraid of flying. These people worry obsessively that they will crash. In extreme cases, a person will have a panic attack. Panic attacks may include shortness of breath, chest pains, nausea, or dizziness.

With the exception of school phobia, most phobias usually develop in the late teens to early adulthood. Women are more likely to suffer from phobia than men. No one is sure why. The best treatment for phobias is exposure to the feared object or place.

Stress

Try This

Write about a time when you were so worried about something that you just couldn't get it out of your mind. What triggered these worries? Did you try to stop worrying? Were you able to do anything that helped? Did your worrying lead to more general feelings of anxiety, so that you found yourself edgy about other things? Try to explore some of the deepest feelings you had connected to this worry. Don't be concerned about punctuation or grammar, just let yourself go. You are writing just for yourself here, you do not need to show it to anyone else.

WHAT'S GOING ON?

Worrying and anxiety can increase stress in our lives which leads to some unhealthy consequences. Writing can relieve you of some of these consequences.

Remember, when we are stressed, the chemicals or hormones associated with the fight-or-flight response are released into the blood stream. The long-term result of this is not good for the body. Research has associated stress with a variety of unhealthy consequences: weakening the immune system, increasing the onset of diabetes, worsening an asthma condition, and triggering episodes of inflammatory bowel disease - to name just a few.

A weakened immune system increases our vulnerability to colds, the flu, and other viral diseases such as herpes.

While many of these medical conditions will require treatment from a doctor, there is something all of us can do to help reduce worry, anxiety and stress. J.W. Pennebaker, Ph.D., of the University of Texas pioneered research into the positive health effects of writing. Others have conducted similar studies, and they all seem to indicate that writing about things which are troubling you boosts the immune system and can lead to better health.

On his website, Dr. Pennebaker gives the following instructions:

Over the next four days, I want you to write about your deepest emotions and thoughts on the most upsetting experience in your life. Really let go and explore your feelings and thoughts about it. In your writing, you might tie this experience to your childhood, your relationship with your parents, people you have loved or love now, or even your career. How is this experience related to who you would like to become, who you have been in the past, or who you are now?

Many people have not had a single traumatic experience but all of us have had major conflicts or stressors in our lives and you can write about them as well. You can write about the same issue every day or a series of different issues. Whatever you choose to write about, however, it is critical that you really let go and explore your very deepest emotions and thoughts.

Warning: Many people report that after writing, they sometimes feel somewhat sad or depressed. Like seeing a sad movie, this typically goes away in a couple of hours. If you find that you are getting extremely upset about a writing topic, simply stop writing or change topics.

http://homepage.psy.utexas.edu/homepage/Faculty/Pennebaker/ Home2000/WritingandHealth.html

You only need to write for about 15 minutes daily for 3-4 days to experience the benefits of this experience. Pennebaker also notes that you do not have to save your work. You can choose to save what you have written or destroy it after the 4-day period.

Did You Know?

A recent study demonstrated that looking out of a window at scenes of nature is a more effective way to relieve minor stress than watching TV. The heart rate of people looking at a natural scene had decreased more than those that watched TV. In fact, watching TV had no more effect on decreasing stress levels than sitting and staring at a blank wall.

Avoid Misunderstandings

Try This

Consider this: You walk into your school cafeteria at lunch and notice that your girl/boyfriend is talking to a classmate of the opposite sex. As you get closer, the classmate leaves. Your girl/boyfriend turns around and appears worried.

Make a list of all the possible reasons your friend looks worried. Ask friends or relatives for suggestions and add to your list.

WHAT'S GOING ON?

In making my list and talking to others, I found everyone could think of at least two reasons why your friend might be worried. This demonstrates that we may be able to recognize a facial expression, but we can't always be sure of the source of emotion. Was your friend worried because s/he may secretly want to date this other classmate and you might find out? Or, is s/he worried because s/he was just informed about a sick friend from elementary school? Initially, we just don't know, so we need to avoid jumping to conclusions which could cause misunderstandings.

We also need to keep in mind that many people want to keep their emotions private. We need to remember to be respectful of the feelings of others. Being able to identify what another is feeling from their expressions doesn't tell us why they are feeling that way, and it doesn't give us the right to call attention to it in many circumstances.

Of course, we would behave differently with someone we are close to. While we may not want to probe a casual acquaintance, it's often okay to check in with a close friend or family member. Even so, we want to be respectful. If something like the above scene were to happen to you, you might want to say something like, "You seem to be a little worried about something. Do you want to talk about it?" As always, we need to be prepared for the person to say no - and the emotional response this may trigger in us!

Key Ideas in Chapter 5

Compare and contrast the facial expression of fear to the facial expression of anger. Place a photo of each side by side, or make a sketch of each side by side. Write lists comparing and contrasting distinguishing features.

Keep it in Mind

Try the following activities to help you learn to recognize when you are afraid and/or worried.

A. Think about a time when you were afraid. Make the face associated with fear to help. Do your best to relive the moment. Remember as many details as possible. Pay attention to how your body feels. When we are afraid, our hands may get colder and our breathing may become deeper and more rapid. You may begin to sweat or feel a trembling or tightening of the muscles in your arms and legs. Take note of these or any other bodily sensation that you experience.

3. Do the same activity for a time when you were worried about something or someone. Try to find a quiet place for this activity. You will probably find that the bodily sensations are subtler (not as noticeable or intense) than when you are afraid. Take note of what you feel like when you are worried.

When you have completed the above activities, make a list of the situations that trigger your fear or worries. Learning to recognize when you are afraid or worried and what your own triggers are provides you with the opportunity to make appropriate reappraisals to direct your actions in the best way. With practice, it will give you the opportunity to modify your emotional reactions. You will be more in control.

6 SURPRISE AND DISGUST

"I was disgusted when I had to dissect a squid. It was weird because it was dead and it was just lying there. It smelt really bad. The teacher said that it was bought from a supermarket and was going to be food if they didn't buy it. It felt really weird. It was slimy and squishy. We had to cut it open with scissors. The interior organs of the squid were all inside a big slime ball, like there was slime in the middle of the squid and the organs were placed inside the slime. The eyes were really squishy. We had a girl squid. You could see the eggs. We saw the heart and liver. The head of a squid is slightly attached to the rest of the body and the fins. We had to pull the head off the squid which was really gross. After we were done the teacher let us do whatever we wanted to do with the squid. It was pretty fun but gross at the same time."

– Caleb

Surprise

Try This

Look at the pictures below. The one on the left is neutral, the other is showing surprise. Make a list of the distinguishing characteristics of the surprise facial expression.

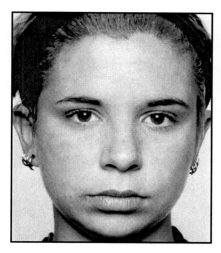 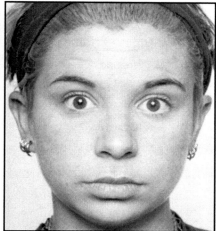

What's going on?

When a person is surprised, we observe the following distinguishing facial characteristics:

o The eyebrows are raised and curved.

o Horizontal wrinkles appear on the forehead.

o The eyelids open and the whites of the eyes are more visible, especially at the top of the eye above the iris.

o The jaw drops without tension in the mouth.

Surprise is a sudden, brief experience. In the seconds after surprise has passed and we reappraise the situation, other emotions will emerge. These emotions could be anger, fear, or happiness.

Like all emotions, surprise varies in intensity from an intense surprise or amazement to a mild surprise or distraction. A mild surprise may only include a partial facial expression such as the raised eyebrows.

Your Turn

Because surprise passes so quickly, it is difficult to find photos of it. Scan your photo collection or a friend's to see if you have one of these rare finds. Look carefully at those from surprise parties. Did the photographer capture the surprise expression, or did the photo show the emotion that followed?

More Fun

Look through magazines or search the internet for posed pictures of surprise. What other nonverbal expressions accompany the surprise facial expressions? Can you find any similarities with other emotions?

Try This

Take a poll of friends and family. Find out how many like surprises and how many do not. If people tell you, "It depends," find out which type of surprises they like and which they do not.

WHAT'S GOING ON?

Surprise is one of those emotions that show the difficulty in trying to classify emotions as pleasurable or not pleasurable. While the circumstances often will determine if a person finds a surprise pleasurable or not, some people do not like surprises of any kind.

A response that is often confused with surprise is the **startle response**. Startle is a physical **reflex** that cannot be suppressed. It is a reflex like the one the doctors test when they tap your knee or elbow with the little rubber hammer during annual exams. Surprise and startle differ in one very key way. You cannot be surprised if you are tipped off ahead of time; you will be startled even if you know what is coming. You may be able to reduce your reaction, but you cannot eliminate it. A sudden loud noise will still produce a startle response even if you know it is coming.

Disgust

Try This

Conduct this **thought experiment** suggested by psychologist Gordon Allport. A thought experiment is when you are asked to imagine and not actually do. Think first of swallowing the saliva in your mouth and then swallow. Note your response to this request.

Now imagine spitting your saliva into a glass and drinking it. How would you respond to this request? Conduct this thought experiment with others and note their reaction.

WHAT'S GOING ON?

Most people will find the second request disgusting. While our mouths produce saliva all the time and we continuously swallow that saliva, once it leaves our body we consider it alien and avoid contact. This response is intensified if the bodily product belongs to another.

Try This

Ask ten to twenty friends or relatives what disgusts them. Write down their answers. (While you are at it, take note of their facial expressions and any other verbal or nonverbal expression. Save this info. We won't be focusing on it right now.) Ask a friend to do the same thing with other people.

What's going on?

Psychologist Paul Rozin and his associates have researched the emotion of disgust. He has identified two large categories of things that disgust people:

- **Core disgusts** include bodily products: feces, vomit, urine, mucus, and blood.
- **Interpersonal disgusts** are triggered by the strange, the diseased, the unfortunate and the morally tainted.

Core disgusts seem to be more innate and universal across cultures. There would seem to be some very obvious health reasons why a person would be repulsed from bodily products.

Interpersonal disgusts are learned and vary more widely from culture to culture. Even within one culture there can be a wide variety in defining what is strange or morally wrong.

Disgust is not just provoked by the sense of sight. We also respond to things that taste and smell bad.

Review the answers you collected in the previous activity; recategorize your responses into "Core" or "Interpersonal." How many do you have for each category?

Try This

Look at the pictures below. Using the neutral one on the left as a guide, make a list of the distinguishing characteristics of the facial expression for disgust shown in the one on the right.

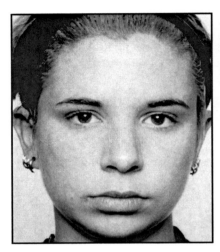 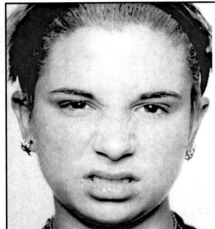

What's Going On?

Disgust is shown largely in the lower face and the eyelids. The distinguishing characteristics of the facial expression for disgust are:

o The upper lip raises and the lower lip raises.
o The nose wrinkles.
o The cheeks raise.
o The eyebrows lower.

Loathing (strong dislike) is a more intense form of disgust, and **boredom** is a less intense form. Disgust can be blended with other emotions to communicate other feelings. Disgust mixed with surprise seems to express disbelief.

Research indicates the universal similarities of the facial expression for disgust across cultures. It is likely that disgust involves a response of getting away from or getting rid of something. It may have evolved, at least in part, as a reaction to danger. Bad food smells and tastes disgusting, so we avoid it and prevent ourselves from getting sick. Sick animals and people often smell or look disgusting, and this reaction probably evolved to ensure that our ancestors kept away from contagious disease.

Your Turn

Keep an eye out for expressions of disgust in magazines and on TV. Make a list and see what the expressions have in common. If you have already made a list with the earlier activity, review your results.

Peculiarly Disgusting

Although our expressions for disgust seem to involve moving away, humans seem to have an interesting fascination for the disgusting. Consider best-selling children's books like *Captain Underpants* and *Garbage Pail Kids*. Other examples of this fascination can be found in the jokes that we tell. We even have a name for this type of joke, we call it "bathroom" humor or "toilet" jokes. How many times have you watched someone pick their nose or pull on bunched underwear for a laugh on TV or in the movies?

Cable TV travel and food channels now regularly include shows where the host travels around the world eating strange foods. These shows all emphasize the host's heroic efforts to overcome feelings of disgust.

Unfortunately, these same responses that are used to entertain us can contribute to feelings of **prejudice** against those with cultural differences. Interpersonal disgust is triggered by the strange or the misfortunate. It is one thing to be disgusted by someone's behavior or choice of food, and quite another to extend that to everything a person does. Historically, different cultures have used this to put down others as less than human or uncivilized. Similarly, we may find ourselves avoiding someone with a physical disability. If we can recognize this trigger, we might be able to reappraise our response in order to see beyond the misfortune and get to know a person who is different.

On the other hand, the closer we feel to the other person, our threshold for tolerating what we would otherwise consider disgusting rises. This is most obvious when we consider the core disgusts and the handling of bodily waste. Parents will have less difficulty changing a diaper or cleaning the food messes of their own children than of a stranger's child. Spouses find it easier to take care of a sick spouse than a stranger. Even the act of kissing seems to underscore this. Some forms of kissing involve exchanges of saliva which, as our opening thought experiment demonstrated, would be unthinkable under normal circumstances.

Did You Know?

Kissing unleashes neural and chemical messages that transmit tactile (or touch) sensations, feelings of closeness, motivation, and/or sexual excitement. A kiss may communicate subconscious information about the compatibility of two people. In some cases, a bad first kiss has cut short a couple's future. Kissing may have evolved from a primate mother's practice of chewing food for her infant and then feeding it to the infant mouth to mouth.

("Affairs of the Lips," Chris Walter, *Scientific American Mind*, 2/2008)

Key ideas in Chapter 6

1. List three distinguishing facial characteristics of surprise.

2. Name two emotions related to surprise.

3. List three distinguishing facial characteristics of disgust.

4. List the two types of disgust.

5. Explain how disgust can keep a person safe.

6. Explain how disgust can be misused to promote prejudice.

95

KEEP IT IN MIND

For the next few days keep a log of when you or the people around you express disgust. Write down the incidents and label the triggers as core or interpersonal. Notice how often disgust figures into a joke being told. Pay particular attention if you notice examples of disgust being used to justify putting down another person.

7 SADNESS

"Today I was sad because I went to the dentist and found out that I had to get braces. I was sad when the dentist said I will HAVE to get braces. It is kind of weird thinking that I will have metal in my mouth for months at a time. I will have to get them tightened and I heard that it hurts."

– Caleb

Triggers for Sadness

Try This

Make a list of things that make you sad. Ask friends and relatives and add to your list of sadness triggers.

What's Going On?

Sadness is triggered by many types of loss. One of the greatest losses someone can face is the death of a loved one. But, the loss does not have to be as permanent as death to make us sad. We feel sad when we lose a friend that has moved to another town, and when a parent has to leave for a long time for a job or because of a divorce. If a friend rejects us, we're sad. We feel sad when we have lost **self-esteem** (feeling confident and good about ourselves).

Sadness is a long-lasting emotion and varies in intensity. We can feel disappointed or distraught, pensiveness or grief, discouraged or despair, sorrowful or miserable. If we are sad for a long time, we might say that we are in a **"blue mood"** or are "depressed." The use of the word "depressed," commonly used by people to describe feelings of being "down" should not be confused with the use of the words by doctors to describe a particular emotional disorder or illness. (We will talk about this disorder later in the chapter.) A person with a sad temperament is said to be **"melancholy."**

Sadness frequently mixes or blends with other emotions, and often sadness will blend with anger. When a person is sad, they tend to lose the will to act, becoming angry helps a person regain the emotional energy needed to do something.

EXPRESSIONS OF SADNESS

TRY THIS

Look at the photos below. The one on the left is neutral, and the one on the right shows sadness. Identify and list the distinguishing characteristics of the facial expression for sadness.

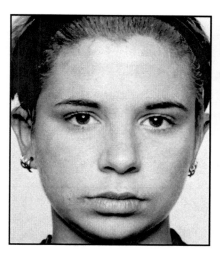 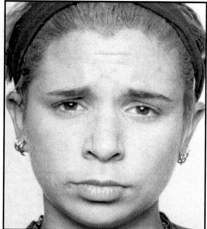

WHAT'S GOING ON?

Sadness is universally recognized. The distinguishing characteristics are:

o The eyes look downward and the upper eyelids droop.

o The corners of the lips are pulled down. The mouth may droop open.

o The cheeks are raised creating a squint and there is tension between the cheeks and the lips which are drooping down.

Your Turn

Look in the mirror and try to make the sad face. Get familiar with what it feels like. Think about something sad to help you. Go back and make some of the faces in the previous chapters to contrast how each feels.

Try This

Get a group of friends together and create a sadness scene and tableau. This is a group activity where people act out a sad scene and then freeze. One person does not participate but acts as the "photographer." This person notes down all the nonverbal expressions and display signals the others reveal. Try this activity several times until you have a good list.

What's going on?

Besides the universal facial expressions, other nonverbal expressions may vary more widely from one culture to another. Some features you may have noticed are dropping the head, lowering of the shoulders, or a general sense of appearing weighted down. Hand positions vary in expressing extreme sadness, such as dropping to the side, covering the face, holding the head or pulling hair.

Also, crying is common when people are sad. However, you should be cautioned that some people cry when they are feeling angry or frustrated, too.

It would be a misjudgment to assume that crying always indicated sadness. Tears sometimes even accompany laughter.

Did You Know?

Color symbolism also varies widely across the globe. Whereas in the United States and other Western European cultures it is common to use black to express death, white is commonly used to express death in East Asian cultures of Japan and China. In South Africa, red is the color of mourning; in Egypt it is yellow. In Thailand purple is worn by widows during mourning.

In the Western cultures, blue is used to express depression and sadness while in Iran it represents spirituality and heaven. See more about color symbolism on this site:

http://webdesign.about.com/od/color/a/bl_colorculture.htm

Your Turn

Experiment with verbal expression and tone to convey different emotions. Choose a common phrase such as "I'm sorry." Repeat this phrase changing your tone to reflect different emotions: fear, anger, disgust, and sadness. Experiment with other phrases. Try to make the facial expression for each emotion as you say the words. Describe the changes in your tone of voice.

More Fun

Make a scrap book of photos of expressions of sadness. Organize these expressions from least intense to most intense. Additionally, try to find photos that contain blends of sadness and other emotions.

Functions of Sadness

Try This

Try to remember a time when you were not really sad but pretended to be sad. What was the outcome? Were you trying to get another person to do something for you? If you can't think of a time, ask a friend or relative if they can recall such a time. You may find that others are reluctant to admit being deceptive (or trying to mislead someone). But if people are willing to be honest, you may find that such deceptions are more common than we care to admit.

What's going on?

An important function of sadness is to arouse others to provide us with help or comfort. Few parents can resist responding to their baby when their baby is crying. Signs of sadness or distress can also motivate us to come to the aid of strangers. This impulse to reach out and help others is important in building and maintaining our sense of community.

For this reason, we may, also, pretend to be sad to get someone to do something for us. Perhaps you have heard the expression "puppy dog eyes"? This is an expression used when someone is obviously displaying sadness to indicate that they want someone to do something for them.

However, not everyone will respond positively when sadness arouses them to help others in need. Some people may feel that an unwelcome demand is being made on them. If we feel as if an unwelcome demand is being made, we are likely to respond angrily. We might put the person down for being weak or unable to care for him/herself. If seeing others as being weak makes you feel more powerful, you may encourage another's suffering.

Have you ever found yourself getting angry with someone who seemed sad? Perhaps you were unconsciously feeling frustrated because you were unable or unwilling to comfort a friend.

Depression

Did You Know?

Shopping when sad is not good for your budget. A recent study published in *Psychological Science* shows people spend more when they are sad. When sad, people become more self-focused and tend to devalue themselves and their current possessions. Spending money seems to relieve these feelings temporarily. (See References for details on the article by Cryder, et al.)

Clinical depression is more than being in a down mood. It is an emotional disorder that leads to a feeling of overwhelming sadness that makes it difficult for a person to carry out their day-to-day activities. A person suffering from clinical depression should consult a medical professional about the best course of treatment. Environmental and biological factors can contribute to depression. Before a clinician can diagnose a person as depressed, four of the following symptoms must be present every day for two weeks:

o Loss of interest and pleasure - the depressed person usually withdraws from people and activities.

o Appetite disturbance - usually this is a loss of appetite causing a significant change in weight.

o Sleep disturbance - usually people find it difficult to fall asleep although sometimes people will want to sleep all day.

o Psychomotor disturbances - people find it difficult to sit still and pay attention.

o Decrease in energy level - people feel tired all the time even if they did sleep or weren't working.

o Sense of worthlessness - this can vary from feeling inadequate to totally worthless.

o Difficulty concentrating - thinking seems to be slower and a depressed person has difficulty making decisions. They are easily distracted.

o Thoughts of death - a depressed person is preoccupied with death and may have suicidal thoughts.

o Associated symptoms - a depressed person may also experience anxiety, phobias, tearfulness and irritability.

Some studies suggest that as many as one in five teens may experience some level of depression. Some symptoms more particular for teens are:

o Poor performance in school

o Anger and rage

o Overreaction to criticism

o Feelings of being unable to satisfy ideals

o Poor self-esteem or guilt

o Substance abuse

o Problems with authority

To avoid feeling depressed, a teen may experiment with drugs or alcohol or become **sexually promiscuous**. Some teens also may engage in **risk-taking behavior**. But such behaviors only lead to new problems: troubled relationships with friends, family, school officials, the law and a deeper depression.

Martin Seligman and his team have spent 40 years studying the subject of children who became depressed to find out why some children become depressed and some do not.

If something goes badly for you, Seligman suggests that blaming yourself does not automatically open you up to feeling sad or depressed. After all, you might think "yeah, it was my fault; but who cares? I don't!" Instead, he discovered that young people were more likely to become depressed if they do one or more of the following things:

o Take setbacks personally (in other words, they think "this means there must be something wrong with me").

o Treat the setback as a disaster that will affect them forever.

o Believe there's nothing they can do about it.

On the other hand, young people who do not see a setback as proof that they are a bad or stupid person tend not to become depressed. Rather, they treat the setback as only one bad thing among lots of good things, or see the situation as temporary and solvable.

So, each of us has a style of thinking that will determine:

o how personally we take it when something goes wrong

o how much of our life we allow the setback to affect

o how long we expect the bad situation to go on for

Challenging **pessimistic thoughts** (thoughts that nothing will turn out right) seems to be a key component to short-circuiting low-level depressions. Here are ways we can learn to challenge pessimism:

o Recognize the thoughts that provoke bad feelings.

o Take a calm look at these thoughts to decide how accurate they really are.

o Learn not to trust thoughts which say that a problem cannot be solved or that things will never get better. Reframe these thoughts: "I'm not smart enough" can become "I've got to study a little harder for the next test."

o Take small steps to achieve a goal. Small steps that are achieved will help reinforce success and make you feel better. If you scored a D on an English exam, don't press yourself to get an A all at once. Set a realistic goal of getting a C and build on this.

Your Turn

One of the leading causes for prolonging a blue mood is ruminating on it (turning it over and over in your mind). Immersing yourself in your sadness only seems to make it worse. Such worries can take different forms from thinking about what is making you sad to focusing on one of the symptoms such as always feeling tired. Instead of ruminating on what's got you down, take some time to get your mind off of it. Take some time now to make a list of some things you might do to get your mind off of what could get you down. Make it as long as possible while you're feeling OK!

If your list included going out with family or friends, when you do so, make sure you don't spend all the time talking about what's got you down.

You also might try writing about what is on your mind. Look again at the Pennebaker activity in Chapter 5 for one way to approach this.

Did You Know?

While careful to point out that depression is not good for people, author Eric Wilson, *Against Happiness*, writes that only by experiencing sadness can we understand what it truly means to be human. He points out research by Ed Diener which shows that when you are in a negative mood, "you become more analytical, more critical and more innovative. You need negative emotions, including sadness to direct your thinking."

KEY IDEAS IN CHAPTER 7

Fill in the blanks.

1. Sadness is often triggered by _____.

2. Two related emotions are _____ and

_____.

3. When sad, the eyes usually look _____.

4. The facial expression for sadness shows a tension created by the

_____ and _____.

5. Sadness is a _____-lasting emotion.

6. An important function of sadness is to _____.

7. Two symptoms of depression in teens are _____ and

_____.

8. Drug use may be a result of _____.

9. Challenging _____thoughts can short-circuit

depressions.

10. Ruminating often _____blue moods.

KEEP IT IN MIND

Sometimes we will find ourselves having an emotional response to another person's mood. This is especially true, as we noted, with sadness, but can occur just as likely with other emotions. Take note of how you respond when you notice that someone is sad. Do you try to comfort or do you withdraw? Keep in mind that neither response may be appropriate. The other person may be unaware that they are expressing this emotion. Be careful about bringing it to their attention. Some people are reluctant to show or discuss their feelings of sadness. Besides, your friend may be going out with you to take his/her mind off of it.

"Usually on Mondays in P.E., we have to run a mile and we get all sweaty and tired. In a happy surprise we got to play baseball today. Baseball doesn't make you sweaty or really tired. In another happy surprise, we won the game because I hit in two runs. I was pretty proud of myself."

– Lauren

Try This

Make a list of happy memories. Try to list at least ten memories that you would consider happy. After you have made your list, examine your memories for similarities. Try to put these memories in different categories and label those categories.

Your Turn

Review the above list and list one or two examples for each kind of happiness from your own life. If you cannot find an example from your own life, ask a friend or relative for an example.

What's going on?

Happiness is that one emotion that we typically think of as positive. But researchers do not agree that happiness is a single emotion. Researcher Paul Ekman suggests that happiness or enjoyable emotions should be categorized separately. According to Ekman, the following are the different kinds of happiness:

o **Sensory pleasures** - These are the feelings we get when we see, hear, taste, touch, or smell something good. One example is the feeling we get when we eat our favorite meal.

o **Amusement** - We are amused by jokes or the antics of a pet. One goal of the entertainment industry is to amuse us.

o **Contentment** - This is a relaxed feeling we get when every thing seems right and there is nothing we feel we need to do. You may feel content on a summer afternoon relaxing in a local park.

o **Excitement** - We get excited by new and challenging situations. Many would consider many of the attractions at an amusement park exciting.

o **Relief** - We feel relief when we find out that we did not fail that difficult math test.

o **Wonder** - Wonder may be felt when we stare out over a city from a tall building. We may feel wonder at the Grand Canyon or another National Park. Wonder causes us to feel goosebumps, sigh, shake our heads, or say "Wow."

o **Ecstasy** - This is an intense feeling sometimes referred to as "rapture" or "bliss." It is often used to describe an extreme religious feeling.

o **Gratitude** - We feel gratitude when somebody does something to help us out.

Ekman also describes three pleasurable emotions identified by other cultures without equivalent words in English. You may not recognize the words, but you will probably have no problem recognizing the feelings being described.

Fiero **(Italian)** - This is the feeling we get when we have met a challenge and done very well. An athlete who has won a grueling match may feel this way. A student who studied hard and got an A on an especially difficult exam may feel this way. It is more than feeling satisfied or prideful. It is common nowadays to pump your fist when you are feeling this way.

Naches (Yiddish) - This is the feeling parents feel when their children have accomplished something. Parents may feel this at graduation, or after a dance recital, or after their child has hit the winning home-run in a Little League game. It is more than just feeling proud of your child. It's the pleasure an adult, particularly a parent, feels when a child excels or does well.

Schadenfreude (German) - This is the feeling of enjoying the misfortune of our enemies or rivals. It is often disapproved by people in our society. While often we are reluctant to admit to this feeling, these feelings are accepted in the sports world. This is the feeling some people have when they root against perennial winners like the New York Yankees or the New England Patriots.

EXPRESSIONS OF HAPPINESS

TRY THIS

Look at the pictures below. Using the neutral one on the left as a guide, identify the distinguishing features for expressing happiness.

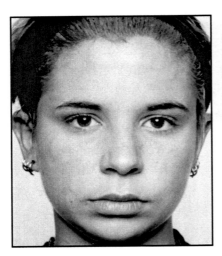 

WHAT'S GOING ON?

Happiness is recognized all around the world. The distinguishing characteristic are:

- o The corners of the lips draw back and up.
- o The mouth is upturned in a smile. The mouth may or may not be opened.
- o The cheeks raise causing wrinkles from the edge of the mouth to the nose.
- o Laugh lines or wrinkles appear at the outer corners of the eyes.

Your Turn

Make a list of other verbal and nonverbal expressions of happiness. It is not uncommon for slang expressions and hand gestures (shaking, slapping) to pass quickly into and out of fashion. These gestures are not universal but very specific to particular groups or sub-cultures. What slang expressions or hand gestures are used by you and your friends in the neighborhood or at school? How widespread are these gestures?

Try This

Look at the pictures below. Which one shows a real smile of happiness and which one is the fake smile?

 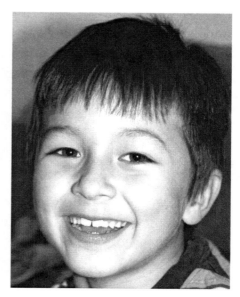

Fake smile at left, real smile at right

What's Going On?

Smiling when we are not happy is not uncommon. We may pretend to smile in amusement because we don't want to insult someone who is trying to be funny. We may fake a smile to try and cover-up another emotion such as anger or fear. Sometimes we smile ironically, trying to communicate that we are not happy. Usually we can tell when a person is faking it, but not always. The difference between a real smile of happiness and a fake smile involves the muscles around the outer portions of the eye. These muscles are responsible for the following differences. In the real smile of a happy person:

o The cheeks are higher.
o The outline of the cheeks has changed.
o The eyebrows have moved down slightly.

These muscles are very difficult to control voluntarily. While some actors can be trained to control these muscles, others simulate enjoyment by actually recalling a happy memory. Thinking happy thoughts can provoke an emotional response and activate these muscles.

Your Turn

Look in the mirror and observe the difference between a real and a fake smile. To provoke a real smile, remember to review your list of happy moments in your life.

More Fun

Look through a photo album. Compare the smiles of people in the photographs. How many photos contain people who were smiling because they were happy? How many people were just "cheesing" it?

DID YOU KNOW?

Research has finally confirmed what TV producers have known for years, that people laugh more when they hear others laugh. Humans are primed to imitate the behavior of other people, especially laughter. Laughter is contagious. This explains why many TV shows play "canned" laughter at the punchlines of jokes. When positive sounds such as laughter are played, the area of the brain responsible for muscle movement becomes active preparing people to smile. Researchers suggest that this behavior promotes social interaction and helps create a stronger sense of community.

http://www.livescience.com/health/061212_contagious_laughter.html

On a personal level, laughter is good medicine. Recent studies suggest that laughter expands the lining of blood vessels and increases blood flow. This is good for your heart and health.

http://www.umm.edu/news/releases/laughter2.htm

Happy and hopeful people or **optimists** also are considerably more likely to survive a heart attack. In a study that evaluated 122 men,

25 were rated most optimistic and 25 were rated most pessimistic. Eight years later 21 of the pessimists had died whereas only 6 of the optimists had died.

Even fake laughter seems to be good for you! Sixty seconds of fake laughter can help put you in a good mood. While the brain may know we are faking, the body doesn't and releases the same chemicals as if we were laughing for real.

http://www.theage.com.au/articles/2003/03/31/1048962698891.html

WHAT MAKES YOU HAPPY?

TRY THIS

Write a story about what will make you happy? Think about the short term and the long term. What will make you happy next month? ...next year? ...five years from now? ...ten years from now?

WHAT'S GOING ON?

People often have very different ideas about what will make them happy. We form stories about what will make us happy and carry these stories around in the back of our minds. These stories may include ideas about growing up, going to college, getting jobs, getting married, or getting a car. No one has determined exactly how we establish a life story, but by the time we are adults, we have a set of beliefs, assumptions and expectations about ourselves and the world we live in.

These schemes are basic to the way the mind works and more important than we usually acknowledge because we judge on comparisons, not facts. When our life story for happiness includes doing better than a brother or a sister, we find ourselves feeling unhappy even with a good job and family if we think our brother or sister is doing better. A person may get good grades in school but be unhappy because their story includes starting on a sports team whereas s/he is a second-stringer.

Surprisingly for some, research suggests that wealth, status, and power are not very important ingredients for being happy. Instead, small moments of positive emotion, concentrating on positive present events, and feeling in control matter more.

Try This

Use the following scale to rate happiness. 1 is not happy and 9 is the most happy.

NOT HAPPY   1 2 3 4 5 6 7 8 9   VERY HAPPY

1. How happy are you?

2. How happy do you think most people judge themselves to be?

3. How happy do you think most people would judge themselves to be after they won the lottery?

4. How happy do you think most people would judge themselves to be after a terrible accident in which they lost the use of their legs?

Ask some friends or relatives the same questions. Record their scores. When you are done, average the results. Ask your friends or relatives to answer anonymously. This will encourage them to be more honest if they aren't feeling particularly happy at this time in their lives.

WHAT'S GOING ON?

The average score that most people choose is approximately 6.5. How did your own rating compare to this average? Most people usually assume that winning the lottery will make them very happy, a rating close to or at 9, and that losing the use of their legs will move them down toward Not Happy, a rating close to or at 1.

When studies have been conducted with actual lottery winners and accident victims, these results hold true, but - and this is a big BUT - only for the short-term. It seems that when surveyed after a year, lottery winners rate themselves as only slightly happier than the average person at 6.8 compared to 6.5. Similarly after a year, accident victims who have lost the use of their legs rate themselves as only slightly less happy than the average person: at 6 compared to 6.5.

It seems that we don't experience happiness simply by what has happened to us but by comparing our experience to our assumptions and expectations. Over time, lottery winners adapt to their new riches and their expectations increase. The net effect is that their overall feelings of happiness do not increase.

So, if we want to increase our feelings of happiness, we need to become aware of our shifting judgments and comparisons. With some effort, we can make comparisons that will highlight all that we have vs. what we think is missing.

Try This

Make a list of the "little" things you do on a daily basis that make you feel happy. Review the different kinds of happiness to make sure that your list is as long as possible.

What's Going On?

Many people would like to know how they can be happier. Psychologist Ed Diener conducted a study to find out what was important to feeling happy. Is it necessary to have an intense emotional response, or are little pleasures good enough? Do we need to pursue big events - going on vacation, going to a party, going to a concert - or should we promote frequent small occurrences? What matters more: how positive a person felt or how often a person felt positive?

Diener's research was clear: happiness is a result of how much time a person spends feeling happy, not from the more memorable, less frequent intense moments of feeling really good. Simple day-to-day pleasures are more important to feeling happy. A life filled with many small moments seems to deliver happiness. For some people this could be walking the dog, listening to music, playing a game, participating in a hobby, or enjoying your favorite dessert.

Did You Know?

A recent study showed that happiness can be inherited. It seems some people may have genes that enable them to remain more optimistic during stressful times. This is not the first study that has made a case for a genetic link for **personality traits**. Other studies suggest that there are genes that influence people who are **novelty seekers** or **antisocial**.

KEY IDEAS IN CHAPTER 8

For the following, answer true or false.

1. Happiness covers a wide range of feelings.

2. Contentment is a type of happiness.

3. The mouth is always open when expressing happiness.

4. There is no difference between a fake smile and real smile.

5. Fake laughter is good for you.

6. Being rich and powerful are not necessary to being happy.

7. Comparison judgments influence whether or not we are happy.

8. Lottery winners are much happier than other people over the long term.

9. Having a hobby can make you happy.

10. Frequent, simple pleasures lead to greater happiness.

KEEP IT IN MIND

Review your list of the little things in your life that make you happy. Try to experience some of these simple pleasures everyday. Many of us are pretty busy, so you may have to make it a goal to make time. Don't stress if you are too busy on any day to meet your goal - that would defeat the purpose! Increase your happiness by increasing the little pleasures in your life.

Answers: 1. True, 2. True, 3. False, 4. False, 5. True, 6. True, 7. True, 8. False, 9. True, and 10. True

SECONDARY EMOTIONS

Try This

We have discussed the six primary or universal emotions. Make a list of other emotions you are familiar with. Ask family and friends to add to your list.

What's Going On?

So far we have explored the six primary or universal emotions. These emotions have all been more widely studied by researchers and it has been found that they all have facial expressions with distinguishing characteristics which are universally recognized around the world.

But there are many other emotions or feelings that we experience. There is less agreement among researchers on how to classify these emotions. Some may be considered **blends** or secondary emotions because they are formed by combining two primary emotions. **Remorse** can be used as an example; remorse can be seen as a combination of sadness and disgust. Others are referred to as feelings because they include an emotional response and thoughts about that emotion. **Embarrassment** can be seen as an example of a typical feeling. Embarrassment arises after we get angry with ourselves for doing something we think of as dumb.

123

The following list is of some of the more common secondary emotions or feelings. It is not a complete list, but it is a good start.

PRIDE

This is a feeling similar to joy and to contentment that comes from achieving something. It can also be felt when we see ourselves as being liked and approved of by the people who are important to us. In a way, it's the opposite of **shame** or remorse. Feeling pride can create a sense of loyalty in us to the people who have given us reason to feel this way. It plays a very important part in helping us to work together as a nation and make us feel good about the times when we have to make sacrifices for the good of everyone else.

We can also feel proud of someone else. This means that we approve of them and we feel happy about what they have achieved. This in turn can lead us to feel loyal to them and defend them against anyone who might try to put them down. This is sometimes a really useful feeling and helps to bond us together in our communities. However, it can become unhelpful when we allow our loyalty to someone block out something about them that needs confronting.

Pride - or the need for pride - can also backfire on us if we exaggerate or lie about ourselves as a way of making other people admire us. There's always a risk that we'll be found out, and other people may come to the conclusion that we're boastful. This can lead to our losing the trust of other people and to feeling shame - another emotion.

Envy

Envy is an uncomfortable emotion we feel if we become angry because someone else gets something we want (and don't have yet). It can also happen in us if someone else has better success than we do. Envy works in the opposite way to pride in that we do not feel pleased for the other person, and we can lose our sense of loyalty to them. Envy can be good if it provokes us into competing in a positive way so that we improve things for ourselves. However, it can be very destructive if it prompts us to try to hurt that other person.

Contempt

Contempt is a negative emotion we may experience towards someone else when we dislike and disapprove of them. Unlike envy, the person we feel contempt towards does not necessarily have anything we want for ourselves. Contempt is a version of disgust in that the emotion prompts us to distance ourselves from the other person and not want to be associated with them. Sometimes contempt is provoked when someone disappoints us and shows themselves to be less than we thought they were.

Jealousy

The word "jealous" comes from the Latin word "zealous" which means "enthusiastic." However, jealousy refers to a kind of enthusiasm that is not always good. It is usually used to describe someone who has become fiercely protective over someone else or something important to them. As we shall see in the section dealing with love, we can become jealous if we feel afraid that someone is trying to take away someone we feel attached to. If we're not careful, this can lead us into being aggressive, not only to the person we feel we are competing with, but also towards the person we love because we can come to feel afraid that they are being disloyal. Sometimes people can get so much into the grip of jealousy that they start to misinterpret what other people are saying and doing, and becoming aggressive or afraid for no real reason. This kind of mistrust and suspicion is also called **paranoia**.

BOREDOM

Boredom is an uncomfortable emotion that comes over us when we are not interested in what is happening around us and would rather go and do something else instead. Boredom is a signal that our brain is feeling either underused or being forced to focus upon something it cannot see the point of. The feeling can increase if we are prevented from leaving - for instance by a teacher in a boring lesson - or because we do not wish to hurt the feelings of someone who is boring us with something only they are interested in. We can also feel bored if we want to find something interesting to do but we are not able to. The amount of boredom we feel is determined by how busy we think we should be or how much entertainment we think we are entitled to.

Love

Examples of two different types of love are romantic love and parental love. What we usually refer to as love lasts too long to be an emotion. Emotions are brief, but love can last for years. Love implies a long-term commitment and attachment to another person. Parental love is usually a lifelong commitment, but romantic love may not last that long. Parental love evolved from the need to look after children for a long time. Because so many changes happen to teens both physically, emotionally and situationally, they often "fall in and out of love" regularly in high school. In the United States, over 50% of adult marriages end in divorce. Love may also be confused with lust or desire. In this way it is related to a sensory pleasure.

Another type of love is related to a religious experience. This is another name for the emotion cited in Chapter 8 as ecstasy, bliss, or rapture.

Your Turn

With parent or guardian permission and supervision, conduct an image search on the internet for the different emotions and feelings in Chapter 9. While the expressions are not universal and are more culturally specific, try to identify some distinguishing features. Compare and contrast these expressions to those of the universal emotions. Prepare a scrapbook noting similarities and differences.

More Fun

Advertisers often try to create an emotional response to help sell their products. Look through a magazine and identify which emotional response an advertiser wants to evoke. For example, an ad for liquid body wash features a photo of a bar of soap with hair clinging to it. Which emotion is being evoked and associated with bar soap? In another example, an ad for a clothing company features a dad holding and hugging his daughter. Which feelings does this company want to associate with their clothes? Try to find examples for a variety of emotions.

Key Ideas in Chapter 9

For each emotion or feeling presented in Chapter 9, write about a time in your life when you have experienced that emotion or feeling.

Keep it in Mind

Become familiar with secondary emotions and feelings in the same way that you approached the universal emotions. Choose an emotion to focus on and write in detail about a time you experienced that emotion. Try to identify the triggers for the emotions. Notice how you responded after your initial emotional reaction. Consider the factors important to making accurate reappraisals. Can you identify any verbal or nonverbal expressions you frequently use when responding to this emotion?

Remember to respect other people's emotions and their right to privacy. We may be able to identify the emotion in another, but we can't always be certain of the source. Avoid misunderstandings that come from jumping to conclusions.

MANAGING EMOTIONS

TRY THIS

Count how many times your heart beats in 30 seconds. To do this, you will have to take your pulse. If you don't know how to take your pulse, follow these steps:

1. Place your index and middle finger on the palm side of your wrist below the base of the thumb. Or, place your index and middle finger on your lower neck off to the side of your windpipe.

2. Press lightly until you feel a pulse, the blood pulsing beneath your fingers. You might have to move your fingers around slightly until you feel your pulse.

FYI - Normal heart rates for a 6-15 year old is from 70 to 100 beats per minute. For a person who is older, it is 60 to 100 beats per minute.

When you have finished taking your pulse for a minute, try counting your breath for 30 seconds. Just sit back, relax, and breathe normally counting only the number of times you inhale.

FYI - Breathing rates vary widely depending on age and activity. On average, the breathing rate for a resting 6-15 year old will be between 16-25 breaths per minute. A resting adult will average 12-20 breaths per minute. A strenuously exercising adult will average 35-45 breaths per minute.

WHAT'S GOING ON?

A study conducted several years ago demonstrated a connection between a person's awareness of internal body sensations and **emotional awareness**. In this study, test subjects were asked to listen to 10 beeps and then decide if the beeps were in synch with their heart rate. Those test subjects that were more accurate in determining whether or not the beeps were in synch with their heart rate were also more attuned to their and others' emotional states.

Brain scans taken during the above experiments showed that the same areas of the brain are active when you are deciding how your body feels and what emotions you are experiencing. For scientists it raises the question on whether we first feel fear and then run from a bear. Or, do we instinctively run from the bear and then interpret our bodily sensations as fear - breathing harder, heart beating faster, muscles contracting. For us, it emphasizes the unconscious, automatic nature of our emotional responses - like our breathing and our heart beating. But like our breathing, we can bring our emotional responses into awareness.

We may never be able to control our emotional responses consciously, but we can take steps to manage them. The first step to any effective management system is to become attentive - to pay attention to those persons, places and circumstances that provoke problematic emotional responses.

DID YOU KNOW?

Some people turn to drugs and alcohol to cope with difficult feelings and emotions. Along with the legal and health issues associated with these activities, drugs and alcohol make it difficult for a person to become attuned to their emotions. Because drugs and alcohol alter your breathing and heart rate, you may misinterpret these feelings for an emotional response. If a person learns to ignore these feelings, it becomes more difficult to recognize them in a true emotional situation. Of course, further problems occur because some drugs alter your brain chemistry. Such alterations impede the brain from functioning properly and encourage dependence on foreign substances. Such malfunctioning can persist long after a person stops using.

Try This

Write about a recent incident in which your emotional response may have been a problem. Maybe you overreacted to something said or done, or you may have not reacted strongly enough.

Use the checklist below to address aspects of your response which you may not have thought about. Refer back to the appropriate chapter for more detailed explanation for those ideas that you may not remember well.

o **Emotions Move Us to Act and Direct and Sustain Our Actions** - What actions occurred as a result of your emotional response? [Chapter 1]

o **Emotions Communicate** - What display signals (facial and hand gestures, tone and volume of voice) did you use? [Chapter 1]

o **Fight-or-Flight** - Did you find yourself automatically reacting in one of these two ways without any conscious appraisal of the situation? [Chapter 3]

o **The Trigger** - Can you identify what triggered this response? [Chapter 3] o **Appraising the Situation** - What was your primary appraisal of the situation. Were you able to reappraise the situation or did your initial emotional response continue to direct your thoughts and actions? [Chapter 3]

o **The Past Is Present** - Was your response triggered by a resemblance to a past event? [Chapter 3]

o **Thoughts and Emotions** - Did specific thoughts trigger your emotional response? What were those thoughts? [Chapter 3]

o **Emotions and Mood** - Did your emotions linger and put you in a "bad" mood? Were you already in a "bad" mood and did that mood influence your appraisal of the situation? [Chapters 2 & 3]

What's Going On?

Because emotional responses vary from one person to another person, the first step to managing your emotions is to become attentive, to pay attention and to become familiar with your unique responses. Don't become confused or discouraged because your responses differ from those of your friends. In fact, if you do talk to your friends, you will find that any emotional response will vary in at least four ways:

1. the speed of emotional onset

2. the strength of emotional response

3. how long your response lasts

4. how long it takes before you feel "normal" again

To begin to be attentive to your unique set of emotional responses, review and practice some of the activities suggested in previous chapters.

o Become familiar with your display signals and physical changes in your body when you are emotional. Review the facial photos in Chapters 4-8. Like a stage actor, practice these faces and any other nonverbal gestures you make with your hands and body. Try to relive some past experiences and notice how you feel on the inside. Is your stomach tightening? How is your breathing?

o Try to keep a journal of problematic emotional incidents. Use the checklist provided above in this chapter to help you explore these incidents.

o Pay attention to your triggers. If possible, put together a list of triggers so that you can begin to anticipate those situations that are likely to provoke an emotional response.

o Begin to notice when an incident starts to resemble something from your past. This will help you reappraise your responses.

o Practice identifying emotional responses in others. Use this as a reminder to check in with your own emotional state. Are they reacting to you? Are you starting to mirror or react to them? Remember, as previously discussed in this book, you probably do not want to "call" another on their emotional reactions. The purpose of noticing another's emotional response is to help you manage yours.

ADDITIONAL ACTIVITIES TO HELP MANAGE ANGER

JUST SAY "STOP!"

This simple technique has proven effective and can help you short-circuit angry thoughts. When you notice that you are becoming angry or having angry thoughts, shout at yourself to "Stop!" In most situations you will probably "shout" at yourself quietly, but if you happen to be home alone, shouting out loud could be helpful. Telling yourself to "stop" can allow you the time to reappraise the situation and your emotional response. You can also use this time to check your facial and nonverbal expressions.

Under some circumstances, you might get a close friend or family member to assist you. Give them a signal for them to come over and tell you to "stop."

Don't be surprised if your body is still giving you the signals that you are angry. Remember becoming angry sets in motion a physical release of stress chemicals. It takes time for your body to recover from this release.

After you have "stopped" your angry thoughts or action, focus your attention on something more enjoyable. Think about what you might shift your attention to before you get angry. For some, it might be going home to a pet; for others, it could be a relaxing afternoon in the park.

When you have used this technique successfully, give yourself a pat on the back. Acknowledging successes helps to keep us motivated.

Commit to Listening

When we become angry, we often start to argue and forget to listen. Use this technique to help short-circuit an angry argument. You may be surprised at how quickly a situation that seems to be boiling over will cool to a simmer when one person stops and listens to the other.

If you find yourself in an angry argument, first tell yourself to "stop." Then tell yourself to "listen." Start off modestly, try listening for five minutes. With practice, you will be able to extend this to ten minutes or more. During these five minutes, you will try not to talk back to the other person. Instead, you are trying to understand the other person's point of view. So the other person doesn't think you are ignoring her/him, repeat back in your own words your understanding of the message. Ask if you understand correctly, and give the person a chance to clarify any misunderstandings you have.

You do not have to agree with the other person, and she/he may be unable or unwilling to listen to you. Remember the goal is for *you* to learn to control *your* angry response and improve *your* listening skills. In many cases you will just have to walk away agreeing to disagree.

To help you master the art of listening, practice this technique in a non-hostile situation. Spend five minutes a day with a friend or family member just listening to whatever is on his mind. Reflect back what you have heard in order to confirm that you understand correctly. Take turns and discover how much fun it is just to listen.

Be Assertive, Not Aggressive

Sometimes you will find that your anger is justified because you or someone you know is being mistreated. It's at these times we must be ready to be assertive, but not aggressive. Remember that hostile, aggressive actions are usually met with a similar response and this won't help us accomplish our goal and correct whatever injustice has provoked our anger.

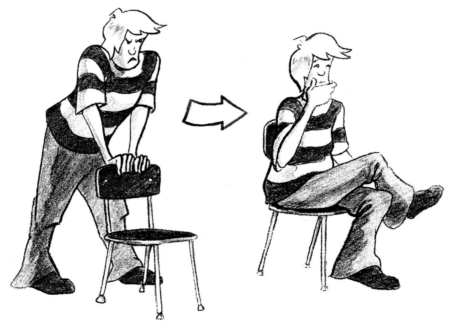

Being assertive takes practice and rehearsal. Keep the following guidelines in mind as you prepare to practice:

o Assertion asks others to change a specific behavior. Limit your request and keep the focus specific.

o Assertive behavior is not hostile behavior. Check your nonverbal and facial expressions. Calmly making a request while sneering will undermine your attempt.

o Try to deliver your request respectfully without raising your voice.

o Avoid overgeneralizing. Don't say, "you never" or "you always." Keep the focus on a specific behavior.

o Make "I" statements. Say, "I feel angry" instead of "You make me angry." Say, "I get angry when you repeatedly remind me to do my homework" instead of "Stop bugging me."

o Outline a specific course of action: "If you continue to ask to copy my homework, I won't go over to your house after school." Or, "I can't concentrate on my homework when you are talking to me. I will talk with you as soon as I am finished."

To begin your practice and rehearsal, look over the trigger list you created earlier in this chapter. Decide which of these triggers requires an assertive response. Use the guidelines above and write down an appropriate response. Practice this response in the mirror or with a close friend. Pay attention to your nonverbal communication.

Try rehearsing these other situations that may not appear on your trigger list:

o Another student "cuts" in front of you on the lunch line.

o Another student keeps interrupting you when you try to answer a question in class.

o Your parent mistakenly accuses you of messing up the kitchen.

o A teammate yells at you for being lazy.

o An older person bullies you.

Even with practice, it may take time before you can replace a **hostile response** with an assertive one. You should also remember that you can't control another's response. You should be prepared to walk away or seek outside assistance. Your ability to control your own hostility may not lead to another person's controlling theirs.

(For more ideas see *Anger Kills* by Redford Williams and Virginia Williams. New York: Harper, 1998.)

Additional Activities to Help Manage Fear

In addition to the Pennebaker writing activity suggested at the end of Chapter 5, the following activities can be helpful in reducing anxiety, stress and worry.

Exercise

Exercise is a good way to relieve stress and anxiety. As little as 30 minutes of exercise three-to-five times a week can be helpful. For maximum benefit, work towards a daily aerobic workout of 30-60 minutes.

CHALLENGE UNHELPFUL THOUGHTS

Worrying is sometimes like a bad habit that is hard to break. One way to short-circuit worrying is to challenge the unhelpful thoughts. To begin:

o Become attentive to the triggers and the physical feelings that are associated with worrying.

o Identify your unhelpful thoughts and beliefs. Do you worry about taking tests, friend's opinions of you, or how you will do in a competition?

o Evaluate the evidence for and against your thoughts and beliefs.

Try making a two-column list, with questions on one side and answers on other. Ask yourself: How often have I done badly on tests? What did my friends say the last time I made a mistake? Or, how do I usually do in this competition?

o Keep a log of your concerns. Go back from time to time and check to see how many of these were justified and how many were without cause. Use your log to help you evaluate the evidence for your thoughts in the future.

ADDITIONAL ACTIVITIES TO HELP MANAGE BAD MOODS AND SADNESS

CHALLENGE NEGATIVE THINKING

People will often keep themselves in bad moods because of the assumptions they make about a situation. When you find that you are in a bad mood because of negative thoughts, challenge that negative thinking by answering some of the following questions:

1. Have I really identified what is bothering me? Try to identify the specific situation that triggered your negative thoughts which led you to feeling bad. This will help you to develop an action plan to deal with that situation.

2. Am I exaggerating the situation? Try to gain a healthy perspective on whatever is bothering you. Ask yourself, "What difference will this make next week, next month, or next year?"

3. Am I overgeneralizing? Don't assume that because something happened once, it will happen again. When thinking about a situation that is getting you down, avoid using words like "always" or "never." Also, be careful with "either-or," "all or nothing," and

"black and white" thoughts. You may have forgotten to do your homework this week, but you can begin to do it next week.

4. Am I overworrying? If you are worrying about something, make sure you have a good reason. If you have a good reason, develop a plan of action. To check how much of your worrying is necessary, make a list of your worries. Check your list from time to time. Notice how most of the things you worried about never happened.

5. Am I assuming the worst? In this situation are you exaggerating the consequences of a particular action?

6. Am I making an unrealistic or unfair comparison? Our minds judge by making comparisons. We need to be careful that those comparisons are fair. Are you comparing your class performance to the top student in the class? Is this fair if you have been a C student in that class? When you judge how well you are doing at sports, are you comparing yourself to a pro athlete or your next-door neighbor?

7. Do I have evidence for my conclusions? Before you jump to conclusions, get the facts. Don't confuse feelings and facts. If you think Tony is mad at you, ask him. If a teacher calls you irresponsible, consider what facts are involved. Have you shown a pattern of irresponsibility or is she/he overgeneralizing?

8. Am I taking it too personally? Accepting responsibility makes sense only when you are dealing with something you can control or influence. Make sure you are not accepting responsibility for something out of your control. Is it your fault your mom's car broke down and you couldn't take your friends to the movies as you promised?

9. Am I discounting the positive? Are you focusing only on the

negative things people say and never hear a compliment? Do you think things like, "She's just saying that to be nice," or "I was lucky," or "Anybody could've done it"?

10. Am I expecting perfection? Give yourself a break. Everybody makes mistakes. Mistakes present opportunities to learn and grow. Being perfect is an impossible standard.

Rehearse Success

When you find yourself feeling down because you aren't happy with how you handled a situation, try rehearsing success:

o   Write down three ways that the situation could have gone better. What alternative actions could you have taken?

o   Write down three ways that it could have gone worse. What actions did you avoid that could have made the situation worse?

o   If you can't think of alternatives that could have improved the situation, think about how someone you respect would have handled a similar situation.

o   Finally, think about what advice you would give someone else if they were facing a similar situation.

Take Action

When you find yourself in a bad mood or feeling down, take action. Don't just think about what you could've done or what you will do. Don't just develop an action plan. Get out there and do something. Nothing feels better than those first small steps - no matter how small. Taking action is the important thing. Doing some simple things can boost your mood. You could decide to clean or reorganize your room. You could go to the library and check out a new book to read or call a friend.

If you are feeling lazy or inadequate, try helping out a friend with his homework. If you have a younger sibling or neighbor, you could try helping them with a school project, or just go out and help them with throwing a baseball or shooting a basketball. If your school has a Kiwans or ACT club that does volunteer work around town, join them and start lending a hand to others. The key is to try to get yourself involved in an activity that will combat your negative thinking and take your mind off yourself and your bad mood.

Don't try to do too much too fast. Start with small steps. If you are facing a larger project, break it down into smaller more manageable steps.

The hardest part is getting started. Don't forget to pat yourself on the back when you do get started. Also, take a moment and try to remember some of your other successes.

(For more ideas see *Mind & Body Handbook* by David S. Sobel and Robert Ornstein. Los Altos, CA: DRX, 1998.)

ADDITIONAL ACTIVITIES TO HELP INCREASE HAPPINESS

As we discovered in Chapter 8, the key to increasing happiness is to increase your experience of simple pleasures throughout your day. Don't put off being happy until you can take that once-a-year vacation. Here are some simple things to try:

- **ENJOY NATURE.** Many studies confirm the positive effect of experiencing natural beauty. Remember the recent study which revealed that just looking out a window at a natural scene lowers stress levels more than watching TV. Find time to go to a park. Take a walk through your neighborhood, down some streets with large trees or nice front lawns. Spend time staring up at the clouds or the stars.

• **BRING NATURE INDOORS.** Try decorating your room with potted plants. If this is not possible, decorate with photos or paintings of outdoor scenes. Better yet, start a collection. Some possibilities are stones, shells, pine cones, or autumn leaves.

• **USE MUSIC TO IMPROVE YOUR MOOD.** Listen to a variety of musical styles to see how music affects your mood. Notice which music makes you sad, relaxed, energized, or happy. Return to that style of music when you want to influence your mood.

• **MOVE TO MUSIC.** Exercise to music to help relieve tension while increasing endurance. Music can help you to get in the mood to exercise more frequently and for longer periods. Upbeat fast tempo music tends to make you feel less tired. Light rock seems to improve endurance and lower heart rates.

o **MAKE YOUR OWN MUSIC.** It is never too late to learn how to play an instrument. Take up a drum, harmonica, guitar, or ukulele to relieve stress, worry, fear or anger. Free instructions for a wide variety of instruments are now available online. You may be surprised how inexpensive some instruments are. If you take a music class in school, you may be able to take one of their instruments home. With a computer, it is even possible to make music without an instrument. Many computers have applications that allow you to create music using tape loops.

• **TAKE A NAP.** Many people think that napping is only for young children or old people, but a short nap of 15-20 minutes can be a great way to improve your mood. When we are tired, we are more often irritable and cranky. As we learned in previous chapters, our emotions influence how we perceive what's going on around us. So take a nap and feel better. If we feel better, the world will look better to us.

• **TAKE A HOT BATH.** A hot bath is a sure way to relax your muscles. Add your favorite bubble bath or scented bath beads with some soothing music for a relaxing experience that appeals to several senses.

• **HAVE A GOOD LAUGH.** Read a joke book or watch a funny movie. Collect cartoons from newspapers and magazines. Share them with friends and family and encourage them to share jokes with you. When you hear a new joke, try to share it with at least five other people. Be on the look-out for humorous situations.

(For more ideas see *Healthy Pleasures* by Robert Ornstein and David Sobel. New York: Perseus, 1989.)

THE BENEFITS OF EMOTIONAL ATTENTIVENESS

Becoming emotionally attentive is sometimes referred to as being **emotionally intelligent**. In the last decade, increasing emotional intelligence has been shown to be highly beneficial. Being emotionally intelligent means you are self-aware, can manage problematic emotions, and are able to feel **empathy** - the ability to understand emotional experiences in others. Employers now regularly seek out employees with these skills, and many schools are starting programs to promote these skills as a way to improve academic performance or test scores.

A student needs to know *how* to learn, not just what to learn in order to succeed. Becoming self-aware, managing problematic emotions, and learning to empathize prepares a student to meet the challenges of school and to meet the challenges of an emotional world.

Additional Classroom Activities

1. **Discussion:** Lead a discussion and ask students to name as many different emotions as they can think of. List them on the board or onto a sheet of paper which can be posted on the wall.

Discuss the fact that facial expressions can bring out emotions in the observer. Ask the students if they know why this is so. Changing one's facial expression can also help to change one's emotion. "Put on a happy face" appears to work. Ask the students if they know why this is so.

2. Ask the students to bring in about 5-10 pictures of people they find in newspapers and old magazines. Put all the pictures into a box and mix them up. Pull out one picture at a time and ask students which emotion they think the person in the picture is exhibiting. Call on several students for each picture. Some students will think a face exhibits one emotion, while others think it expresses another. Emphasize the point that reading people's faces is only one way to determine how a person is feeling. Sometimes people "mask" their feelings with a smile or frown.

3. Listen to samples of different styles of music and notice how they affect people. In small groups, have the students check with each other and compare how they felt. Explore reasons for the differences, and the similarities of their responses. Discuss how students might use music to change a mood, or energize themselves.

4. Obtain a diagram of the structure of the brain and go over the different parts of the human brain. Compare and contrast the human brain to some graphics of animal brains.

5. **Discussion: Snake, dog, fish, fly, gorilla and eagle:** Can snakes feel anger? Pleasure? Can dogs, etc.? Discuss the ways that these animals might "feel." How can we tell what animals might feel or not feel? Perhaps animals feel emotion just like us, but they simply don't show it in a way we understand.

6. **Discussion: Could a computer someday have feelings?** Aircraft warning systems are now being designed to have a voice, with the right level and expression of urgency, telling the pilot about approaching danger. Computer-

generated cartoons have characters that show emotion on their faces. And simple robots can approach what is good for them and avoid what is dangerous. Discuss whether these examples are a start in the direction of computers having feelings. Some people already love their computers, but will computers someday love their owners?

Discuss how our understanding of brain structure argues against the idea that computers will learn to feel. (Use the images of the brain and its parts.)

7. Display Rules in Emotions: Form three groups of students. Assign each group one of the following discussion topics:

Group 1. Social rules control the display of emotion. What are the display rules in class? At home? In public places? What happens when those rules are broken? What would life be like with no emotional display rules at all?

Group 2. We are expected to conform to display rules. Such conformity helps keep a society stable and helps us understand what to do in different situations. Discuss the ways that conforming to social display rules can help us and how conformity can also act as a limiting factor and can stifle our progress.

Group 3. Clothing and other fashion items have been promoted as an expression of personal style, a way to express your personality. It seems that many, if not most, people have accepted that idea. (For example, some people deliberately choose the color of their clothing to reflect their mood, and in the West, black is the accepted color to wear at a funeral.) Consider that fashion is really an extension of your personal expression. Describe ways that clothing "makes a statement," and describe any display rules that might apply to those fashion statements. Do any such personal statements have an emotional aspect? Discuss punk, goth, retro and other fashions.

8. Discussion: Discuss the following quote from Percy Bysshe Shelley, and explore the ways that happiness and sadness are linked:

> We look before and after,
> And pine for what is not,
> Our sincerest laughter
> With some pain is fraught:
> Our sweetest songs are those
> that tell of saddest thought.

9. In groups of three, have the students imagine and act out a complex social situation, such as an apparent "love triangle" or "auditions for a coveted role in a play" or "vying for a spot on a sports team," where one person gets sad, another angry or some other emotion. Ask the larger group for possible explanations for the various emotions. Reveal the "actual" explanation to illustrate that usually we don't know the reasons for someone's emotion.

10. Discussion: Discuss the following quote from Robert Louis Stevenson, and explore the ways that disgust is influenced by social norms.

"Nothing more strongly arouses our disgust than cannibalism, yet we make the same impression on Buddhists and vegetarians, for we feed on babies, though not our own."

11. Writing Assignment: Can money buy happiness? Have the students write a short story comparing the happiness of giving with the happiness of receiving. Suggest that they imagine a situation where receiving money could result in suffering, or imagine a situation where losing all your possessions can result in happiness.

12. Discussion: Can we ever completely hide our emotions? When would it be good to do so? Not so good?

13. Discussion Topics: a. Why do some people like sad stories? **b.** What are your local sadness display rules for men and women? Are they different for men than they are for women? Why do you think so?

14. Discussion Topic: Being Alert!
Contact a local safety expert (a police officer, for instance). Have him/her give a talk on being aware of surroundings at all times, avoiding risky behavior, and seeking help from responsible adults when in uncomfortable situations. (For further information on teaching people to learn to read our own warning flags when danger is near, read *The Gift of Fear* by Gavin De Becker.) Divide the kids into groups of 4-5 and have them discuss situations where they felt something or someone was not quite what it or he/she should be. Tell them these feelings are part of our "early warning system" built into our bodies, and that they can actually rely on these feelings to help them be safe. Ask them to discuss whether these feelings could get out of hand, too, and prevent people from doing anything. (See Ch. 12 on fear and the section on paranoia in Ch. 9, pg. 126.)

15. Conflict-Resolution Activity: This activity can be stretched out to several sessions. After the sessions are over, have each group present their findings and theories to the rest of the class.

Divide the students into groups of 4-6 people, and each group is to pick out a news story, a TV show or movie on or about war. It can be a fictional piece, and it doesn't matter if the groups choose the same story or show. They are to find out what started the war, who the parties are that are involved, why the parties are involved in the conflict, and make a list under each party's name of what their underlying issues are. They may need to look up facts in history books, in other news stories, on the web, and so on. Once this is done, have them take issues on each side of the conflict and try to find nonviolent solutions to them. You should instruct them that an issue may seem to be solvable on one side, but would actually fuel violence on the other side. (For instance, banning a religion or a cultural ritual in a country to keep conflicts at a minimum is an example of a resolution that would not be good for both sides, and may even make the violence worse.)

16. Discussion: Divide the students into groups and have them think of times when they were "bored." Tell them to consider the possibility that other feelings might lurk behind boredom. Was it really boredom, or were they thinking about other things that just got in the way of what they were supposed to be doing or thinking about? Perhaps boredom was caused by lack of sleep, too much or too little to eat, prescription and other drugs. Have them discuss this among their group. They should learn that substituting boredom for some other emotion or state is probably something we all do from time to time.

17. Writing task: Have each student take one of the topics in this book and write a short fiction story about it, and tell them they can include drawings or pictures to help illustrate it. After they turn in their papers, list which topics were chosen and share your results. You may suggest that if more people wanted to write about one certain topic, perhaps it was because this is the emotion that is most prevalent at that moment. It could have been influenced by current news, for instance. Have the students discuss why one emotion topic was chosen over another. If there was an even distribution of topics, have the students discuss why this would be. (All of us have different emotional feelings at different times, which is a healthy thing.)

Glossary of Terms

adrenal glands, located just above each kidney in the lower back and responsible for producing **hormones** the body needs, especially when the **emergency reaction system** is activated.

ambiguous situations, uncertain situations where internal feelings can be similar for different emotions. In ambiguous situations, we are more likely to misinterpret our emotional reactions.

antisocial personality, a disorder that is characterized by a lack of concern or caring for other people.

anxiety, a general emotional reaction, such as worry, that develops in response to anticipating future events.

assertiveness (nonassertiveness), being assertive is where one can defend and state ideas and thoughts without being aggressive or hostile. Nonassertive behavior includes feeling inadequate about speaking up or taking action or not acting for fear of being rejected.

automatic appraisals or **autoappraisals**, our initial and sometimes not conscious understanding of the meaning of an event; some appraisals we are born with (such as fear of the unknown) while others are learned (such as getting angry at an aggressive driver on the freeway).

autonomic nervous system, a part of the nervous system responsible for running internal organs, such as the heart, kidneys, liver and stomach. "Autonomic" means without conscious control.

brain (parts of): **amygdala**, two small sections on either side of the brain that seem to help us be aware of our surroundings, help us mobilize our actions and recognize emotions in other people; **anterior cingulate**, part of the limbic system that sends signals from the amygdala to other systems in the body to start reaction; **cingulate gyrus**, gathers all the incoming information from the outside world and the body and compares all this information with as many memories as it can and sends the information and memory to other parts of the brain; **cortex**, the largest part of the brain which produces most of our human activities, such as language and art; **frontal lobes**, part of the cortex

151

involved in planning and seem to contain different emotions; **hypothalamus**, a pea-sized organ in the limbic system that helps regulate many activities relating to survival, such as eating, sleeping, body temperature, heart rate, hormones, sex and emotions; **limbic system**, an area in the lower center of the brain where emotions are decided upon and generated by sending information to the amygdala to make sure the person can take instant action and also to the upper cortex where complex thinking occurs; **prefrontal cortex**, the part of the brain where we think things in order to react in the right way; **upper cortex**, the part of the brain where we do our complex thinking.

depression (clinical depression), an emotional disorder that leads to a feeling of overwhelming sadness which makes it hard to carry out ordinary day-to-day activities.

disgust (core & interpersonal), sensory input (such as seeing, hearing or smelling) that is considered bad or inappropriate. Two categories are "core disgusts" which include bodily products (feces, vomit, blood, etc.) and these seem to be universal across cultures; and interpersonal disgusts which are learned and vary from culture to culture.

display rules, acceptable ways of expressing emotions, and these rules vary from culture to culture.

display signals (emotional), facial expressions, body movements, hand gestures, language and other signals we use to express our emotions. **Verbal display signals** include words we may have chosen and the way we choose to say them, and **nonverbal display signals** include facial expressions and gestures.

emergency reaction system, the parts of our body that prepare us to respond to sudden, unexpected events. It includes stimulating the production of **hormones** which set off certain reactions, such as the **fight-or-flight response**.

emotional attentiveness or **emotional intelligence**, being self-aware, managing problematic emotions and being able to show **empathy**, the understanding of emotional experience of others.

emotional awareness, being able to bring emotional responses into awareness in order to manage them.

"Emotional Cycle," an emotional response involves a **trigger**, an initial appraisal of a situation, then responding with certain actions (or inactions) which, in turn, give feedback to help with a reappraisal of the situation and further or different action; and the cycle continues throughout the given situation.

emotional disorders, conditions that are apparent when one emotion dominates a person's life making it difficult to carry out basic tasks, such as eating, sleeping or going to work or school. Some examples are extreme forms of **stress**, such as **anxiety**, **panic attacks** and **clinical depression**.

emotional response, the automatic pattern of responding to certain situations. The response is usually **involuntary** (outside of conscious control) and can lead to changes in our body, such as changes in breathing, heartbeats and blood pressure.

emotions, specific involuntary and autonomic patterns of short-lived physiological and mental responses whose purpose is to motivate us to act in situations. The six **primary** or **universal emotions** are anger, fear, surprise, disgust, sadness, and happiness (see also "secondary emotions").

fight-or-flight response, the body's **emergency reaction system** that kicks in when we sense a threat in the environment. The process determines whether there is real danger and, therefore, defensive or evasive measures are called for.

happiness, a positive emotional state, of which there are several categories, such as **sensory pleasures** (feelings from seeing, hearing, feeling something good), **amusement, contentment** (feelings of comfort and that everything is right), **excitement, relief, wonder, ecstasy**, and **gratitude** (the feeling when someone helps us). Happiness can be achieved through **simple pleasures**, such as enjoying nature, listening to music, taking a nap and other relaxing activities,

hormones, also called "**messenger chemicals**," are manufactured by special glands and are carried through the blood to specific targets in the body. Examples of hormones are **norepinephrine**, a hormone that prepares the body to respond to external events, and **serotonin**, a chemical that connects different systems in the brain and is involved in regulating sleep. These chemicals are released when the brain detects **triggers** such as **tactile** (or **touching**) **sensations** or loud and unexpected sounds. (See also "neurons.")

hostile response, a response usually from anger or fear that includes an aggressive, often offensive, action, not often an appropriate response to the situation, such as **road rage**, where one loses control over anger and frustration with traffic. There is a connection between **hostility and health** in that people who are often angry or aggressive are at a higher risk of developing life-threatening diseases.

immune system, our body's defense against infectious organisms and other invaders. Through a series of steps called the **immune response**, the immune system attacks these organisms and substances that invade body systems and cause disease. The immune system is made up of a network of cells, tissues, and organs that work together to protect the body. The cells involved are white blood cells, or **leukocytes**, and they are produced or stored in many locations in the body, including the **thymus** (a small organ in the chest that produces **T-cells** that fight disease), **spleen** (an organ in the abdomen that filters blood to remove disease-causing invaders), **liver** (large organ which helps **glucose**, or sugar, get into the blood stream in order to provide energy to the body) and **bone marrow** (the center part of the bone where blood cells are produced).

involuntary response, emotional or physiological (physical) reactions to a situation that seem to be outside of conscious control. (See also "autonomic nervous system.")

micro-expression, a facial expression or body movement that lasts a second or less when an emotion is activated. These expressions seem to be involuntary. There are experts who have learned to recognize these "flashes" by how the face and body react and thereby know which emotional reaction was expressed, even if it's just in an instant.

mood, long-lasting states of feelings and emotions. A **blue mood** is a longer state of sadness, but should not be confused with an unhealthy state of extreme sadness or **anxiety** called **clinical depression**. A person who has a sad **temperament**, is said to be **melancholy** or "moody." A person who is angry for a long time is said to be in a **bad mood** or foul mood.

negative thinking, thoughts that tend to keep a bad or blue mood going and does not help solve problems. Some negative thinking involves **overworrying**, **overgeneralizing** ("He is always laughing at me..."), **exaggerating** ("This final is never going to end..."), assuming the worst will happen, making unrealistic or unfair comparisons, and taking things too personally.

neuroeconomics, a field of study that examines how our emotions influence how we perceive money and finance.

neurons, nerve cells in the brain and other parts of the body which send messages to each other through electrical pulses sent along chemicals called **neurotransmitters**.

optimists, happy and hopeful people (the opposite of pessimists).

panic attack, an extreme form of anxious thoughts or **anxiety** that is intense and quick to arise. It can begin when someone is feeling stressed and the **amygdala** in the brain signals a **fight or flight response**.

paranoia, a form of **antisocial personality** where there is an extreme distrust and suspiciousness of other people, and sometimes accompanied with feelings of persecution.

personality trait, a general and long-lasting quality of a person's psychological makeup that influences thoughts, feelings, and actions over time and across situations.

pessimistic thoughts, beliefs that nothing will turn out well, which seem to be a key component of low-level **depressions**.

phobia, the Greek word for "fear" and is an extreme or unfounded fear of a specific object, place or situation. Some examples are **acrophobia**, the fear of heights; **agoraphobia**, the fear of open or public places; **aviophobia**, the fear of flying; **claustrophobia**, the fear of closed spaces (elevators, classrooms); and **zoophobia**, the fear of animals.

physiological responses, physical (bodily) reactions to emotions, such as sweaty palms when scared or nervous, increased heart rates when excited, blood pressure changes, eyelids opening or closing when certain emotions are felt, and so on.

prejudice, comes from "pre-judging" others based on the need for our mental system to simplify the world. It can lead, however, to extreme reactions such as "all women are stupid."

primary appraisal, the first, usually unconscious, evaluation of a situation which sets in motion an emotional response. It is part of the "**Emotional Cycle**" and is subject to reappraisal as more information is processed in the brain.

reflex, inborn and unlearned responses to stimuli. The **startle response** is a physical reflex that cannot be suppressed, such as jumping at an unexpected loud noise (balloon bursting, a firecracker going off, etc.).

risk-taking behavior, actions that put an individual and others in danger. Some people have an unhealthy addiction to risk-taking behavior. **Novelty seekers** are people who exhibit a form of risk-taking behavior where they constantly seek new and exciting experiences in order to feel good.

secondary emotions, are either **blends** (combinations) of **primary emotions** or are less biologically-based. Some examples are **remorse** (a combination of sadness and disgust), **embarrassment** (anger at oneself blended with remorse), **pride** (feeling of superiority), **envy** (angry at not having something others have), **contempt** (a form of disgust which prompts people to distance themselves from others, and **hate** and **loathing** are subsets of contempt and disgust), **jealousy** (feelings that cause a person to be fiercely overprotective of someone else or some thing), **boredom**, and **love**.

self-esteem, feeling confident and good about oneself. Low self-esteem is a feeling of inadequacy about one's ability.

sexually promiscuous behavior, unhealthy sexual activities that stem from low **self-esteem**. This **risk-taking behavior** can lead to disease, unplanned pregnancies, injury, as well as legal prosecution, especially if involving a minor.

shyness, a type of fearfulness or **anxiety** about interacting with others that is experienced over a long period of time.

stress, a reaction due to the failure of adapting to change. Stress can happen when internal feelings and external demands seem too great to handle.

stress chemicals, these are **hormones** and other substances made in the **adrenal glands** and released by our body's **emergency reaction system** whenever a stressful event occurs. Some of these chemicals are: **cortisol**, which increases the amount of **glucose** (sugar) in the blood and raises blood pressure to give muscles fuel and helps to delay damage to muscles; **norepinephrine** (commonly called **adrenaline**), which helps to make us more alert and speeds up our actions; **fibrogen**, which thickens the blood to help heal wounds; and **glycogen**, the body's store of glucose used for energy.

temperament, the enduring emotional characteristics of a person.

thought experiment, suggested by psychologist Gordon Allport, is an exercise when you are asked to imagine a situation or action and not actually doing the action or becoming involved in the situation. This experiment was used to help identify facial expressions and other bodily responses to emotions.

triggers (emotional triggers), the events or situations that precipitate or start an emotional reaction. A trigger is the first part of the "**Emotional Cycle**."

writing and health connection, research by J.W. Pennebaker, Ph.D., and others, has shown that when people write about things which are troubling them, this boosts the **immune system** and can lead to better health. However, they do advise that if writing causes more sadness, to stop and change the subject.

References & Further Reading

Cryder, C. E., Lerner, J. S., Gross, J. J., & Dahl, R. E. (2008). Misery is not miserly: Sad and self-focused individuals spend more. *Psychological Science, 19*, 525-530.

De Becker, Gavin. (1999) *The Gift of Fear*. Dell, New York (also Bloomisbury, London (2000))

Diener, Ed & Biswas-Diener, Robert, (2008) *Happiness: Unlocking the Mysteries of Psychological Wealth*, Wiley-Blackwell, Malden, MA.

Ekman, Paul & Friesen, Wallace. (2003) *Unmasking the Face: A Guide to Recognizing Emotions from Facial Expressions*. Malor Books, Los Altos, CA

Ornstein, R., (1991) *Psychology: The Study of Human Experience, 3rd Ed.* Harcourt, New York.

Ornstein, Robert & Sobel, David. (1989) *Healthy Pleasures*. Perseus, New York.

Payton, J., Weissberg, R.P., Durlak, J.A., Dymnicki, A.B., Taylor, R.D., Schellinger, K.B., & Pachan, M. (2008). The positive impact of social and emotional learning for kindergarten to eighth-grade students: Findings from three scientific reviews. Collaborative for Academic, Social, and Emotional Learning, University of Chicago, Chicago, IL.

Pennebaker, J.W. (1997). *Opening Up: The Healing Power of Expressing Emotion*. Guilford Press, New York.

Pennebaker, James.W. (2004). *Writing to Heal: A Guided Journal for Recovering from Trauma and Emotional Upheaval.* New Harbinger Press, Oakland, CA.

Rozin, P., & Fallon, A. (1987). A perspective on disgust. *Psychological Review, 94*, 23-41.

Seligman, Martin, et al. (2007). *The Optimistic Child: A Proven Program to Safeguard Children Against Depression and Build a Lifelong Resilience*. Houghton Mifflin, New York.

Sobel, David S. & Ornstein, Robert (1998) *Mind & Body Handbook*. DRX, Los Altos, CA

Walter, Chris (2008). "Affairs of the lips," *Scientific American Mind*, February 2008.

Williams, Redford & Williliams, Virginia. (1998) *Anger Kills*, Harper, New York.

Wilson, Eric (2008). *Against Happiness: In Praise of Melancholy*. Farrar, Straus and Giroux, New York,

Websites Referenced in Book

http://.movies.com/boxoffice Published by Fandango.com, Los Angeles.

http://IMDb.com Published by IMDb.com, Inc. (an Amazon.com company), Seattle, WA

http://www.andrews.edu/~tidwell/lead689/NonVerbal.html (2003) Charles H. Tidwell, Jr., PhD., Andrews University, Berrien Springs, MI 49104-0801

http://homepage.psy.utexas.edu/homepage/Faculty/Pennebaker/Home2000/Writing andHealth.html (2003) James W. Pennebaker, Department of Psychology, A8000, The University of Texas, 1 University Station, Austin, Texas 78712

http://webdesign.about.com/od/color/a/bl_colorculture.htm Color Symbolism Chart by Culture: Understand the Meanings of Color in Various Cultures Around the World, Jennifer Kyrnin, About.com (part of *The New York Times* Company, New York.)

http://www.livescience.com/health/061212_contagious_laughter.html Laughter Really Is Contagious (2006). Andrea Thompson, LiveScience.com (LiveScience.com is owned by TechMediaNetwork.com, New York.)

http://www.umm.edu/news/releases/laughter2.htm (2005) Miller, Michael, M.D., et al. Laughter Helps Blood Vessels Function Better. University of Maryland Medical Center, University of Maryland, Baltimore,

http://www.theage.com.au/articles/2003/03/31/1048962698891.html Even Fake Laughter is Good Medicine (from *Washington Post* article on the research of Charles Schaefer, Fairleigh Dickinson University, New Jersey)

Index

American Psychological Association National Standards for High School Psychology Curricula

	Ch. 1: What Are Emotions & Why Do We Have Them?	Ch. 2: Clarifying Emotions	Ch. 3: Interpreting Emotions	Ch. 4: Anger	Ch. 5: Fear	Ch. 6: Surprise and Disgust	Ch. 7: Sadness	Ch. 8: Happiness	Ch. 9: Secondary Emotions	Ch. 10: Managing Emotions
II. BIOPSYCHOLOGICAL DOMAIN **Standard Area IIA: Biological Bases of BehaviorExpectation**										
CONTENT STANDARD IIA-1: Structure and function of the neuron										
IIA-1.1 Identify the neuron as the basis for neural communication										
b. Discussing how internal and external stimuli initiate the communication process in the neuron	X	X								
CONTENT STANDARD IIA-3: Hierarchical organization of the structure and function of the brain										
IIA-3.1 Identify the structure and function of the major regions of the brain										
a. Identifying the regions of the brain by using diagrams and/or computer-generated diagrams	X									
b. Summarizing the functions of the major brain regions	X									
CONTENT STANDARD IIA-5: Structure and function of the endocrine system										
IIA-5.1 Describe how the endocrine glands are linked to the nervous system										
a. Discussing the effect of the hypothalamus on the endocrine system	X									
c. Giving examples of how hormones are linked to behavior and behavioral problems		X								
CONTENT STANDARD IIC-2: The role of biology and learning in motivation and emotion										
IIC-2.2 Describe the situational cues giving rise to anger and fear										
a. Analyzing occasions on which they became angry or afraid				X	X					
b. Evaluating personal experiences of discrimination giving rise to fear and/or anger				X	X					
CONTENT STANDARD IIC-6: Physiological, affective, cognitive, and behavioral aspects of emotions and the interactions among these aspects										
IIC-6.2 Explaining how emotions and behaviors are related										
a. Describing how emotions related to non-verbal communication	X			X	X	X	X	X	X	
b. Identifying components of the emotional experience		X		X	X	X	X	X	X	

Web Source: http://www.apa.org/ed/natlstandards.html

California Middle School and High School Health Standards
(Based on the California Framework)

	Ch. 1: What Are Emotions & Why Do We Have Them?	Ch. 2: Clarifying Emotions	Ch. 3: Interpreting Emotions	Ch. 4: Anger	Ch. 5: Fear	Ch. 6: Surprise and Disgust	Ch. 7: Sadness	Ch. 8: Happiness	Ch. 9: Secondary Emotions	Ch. 10: Managing Emotions
Unifying Idea: Acceptance of personal responsibility for lifelong health **Expectation 1:** Students will demonstrate ways in which they can enhance and maintain their health and well-being. **Mental and emotional health:** • Developing and using effective communication skills.			X							X
• Developing and using effective coping strategies, emphasizing strategies for coping with feelings of inadequacy, sadness, and depression.			X							X
Unifying Idea: Respect for and promotion of the health of others **Expectation 5:** Students will understand and demonstrate how to promote positive health practices within the school and community, including how to cultivate positive relationships with their peers. **Friendship and peer relationships:** • Demonstrating acceptable ways to show or express feelings.			X	X	X	X	X			
• Resolving conflicts in a positive, constructive way.			X							X
Unifying Idea: An understanding of the process of growth and development **Expectation 6:** Students will understand the variety of physical, mental, emotional, and social changes that occur throughout life. **Life cycle:** • Managing feelings appropriately.										X
• Developing and using effective communication skills to discuss with parents or other trusted adults the changes that occur during adolescence.										X
Expectation 7: Students will understand and accept individual differences in growth and development. **Mental and emotional development:** • Identifying, expressing, and managing feelings appropriately.	X	X	X	X	X	X	X	X	X	X
• Developing and using effective communication skills.										X

Web Source: http://www.cde.ca.gov/ci/cr/cf/documents/healthfw.pdf

California State High School Life Science Standards

	Ch. 1: What Are Emotions & Why Do We Have Them?	Ch. 2: Clarifying Emotions	Ch. 3: Interpreting Emotions	Ch. 4: Anger	Ch. 5: Fear	Ch. 6: Surprise and Disgust	Ch. 7: Sadness	Ch. 8: Happiness	Ch. 9: Secondary Emotions	Ch. 10: Managing Emotions
9. As a result of the coordinated structures and functions of organ systems, the internal environment of the human body remains relatively stable (homeostatic) despite changes in the outside environment.										
9. b. The nervous system mediates communication between different parts of the body and the body's interactions with the environment	X	X								
9. d. Students know the functions of the nervous system and the role of neurons in transmitting electrochemical impulses	X	X			X					
9. e. Students know the roles of sensory neurons, interneurons, and motor neurons in sensation, thought, and response.	X				X					

Web Source: http://www.cde.ca.gov/ci/cr/cf/documents/scienceframework.pdf

National Board for Professional Teaching Standards - Health

(These standards are for teachers who are attempting to become board certified. The *Me and My Feelings* curricula falls in line with methods teachers can use to show their competency)

	Ch. 1: What Are Emotions & Why Do We Have Them?	Ch. 2: Clarifying Emotions	Ch. 3: Interpreting Emotions	Ch. 4: Anger	Ch. 5: Fear	Ch. 6: Surprise and Disgust	Ch. 7: Sadness	Ch. 8: Happiness	Ch. 9: Secondary Emotions	Ch. 10: Managing Emotions
I. Knowledge of Students — Accomplished health education teachers obtain a clear understanding of individual students, their family structures, and their backgrounds.		X	X	X	X	X	X	X	X	X
II. Knowledge of Subject Matter — Accomplished health education teachers have a deep understanding of the components of health and health content and their interrelationships.	X	X	X	X	X	X	X	X	X	X
III. Promoting Skills-Based Learning — Accomplished health education teachers, through their passion and effective communication, maintain and improve health-enhancing student behavior by delivering health content through skills-based learning.	X	X	X	X	X	X	X	X	X	X
IV. Curricular Choices — Accomplished health education teachers select, plan, adapt, and evaluate curriculum to ensure comprehensive health education.	X	X	X	X	X	X	X	X	X	X
V. Instructional Approaches — Accomplished health education teachers use an array of engaging instructional strategies to facilitate student learning.	X	X	X	X	X	X	X	X	X	X

Web Source: http://www.nbpts.org/userfiles/File/Health_53_STD.pdf

National Board Professional Teaching Standard: Adolescence and Young Adulthood Science Standards

(These standards represent how *Me and My Feelings* can aid a teacher's pursuit in helping students achieve science literacy as described by the National Department of Education)

	Hits Standard Well	Touches on Standard
<u>Preparing the Way for Productive Student Learning</u>		
I. Understanding Students Accomplished Adolescence and Young Adulthood Science teachers know how students learn, know their students as individuals, and determine students' understanding of science as well as their individual learning backgrounds.		X
II. Understanding Science Accomplished Adolescence and Young Adulthood Science teachers have a broad and current knowledge of science and science education, along with in-depth knowledge of one of the subfields of science, which they use to set important and appropriate learning goals.		X
III. Understanding Science Teaching Accomplished Adolescence and Young Adulthood Science teachers employ a deliberately sequenced variety of research-driven instructional strategies and select, adapt, and create instructional resources to support active student exploration and understanding of science.	X	
<u>Establishing a Favorable Context for Student Learning</u> **IV. Engaging the Science Learner** Accomplished Adolescence and Young Adulthood Science teachers spark student interest in science and promote active and sustained learning, so all students achieve meaningful and demonstrated growth toward learning goals.		X
<u>Advancing Student Learning</u> **VII. Fostering Science Inquiry** Accomplished Adolescence and Young Adulthood Science teachers engage students in active exploration to develop the mental operations and habits of mind that are essential to advancing strong content knowledge and scientific literacy.		X
VIII. Making Connection in Science Accomplished Adolescence and Young Adulthood Science teachers create opportunities for students to examine the human contexts of science, including its history, reciprocal relationship with technology, ties to mathematics, and impacts on society, so that students make connections across the disciplines of science, among other subject areas, and in their lives.	X	

Web Source: www.nbpts.org/the_standards/standards_by_cert?ID=4&x=44&y=6

CPSIA information can be obtained at www.ICGtesting.com
Printed in the USA
LVOW051918130212

268548LV00001B/1/P